Ethnic Minority Families

SHARON BEISHON is a Qualitative Methodologist at the Office for National Statistics and is currently working on the development of questions for the 2001 UK Census. She was formerly a Research Fellow at the Policy Studies Institute. Her previous work includes co-authorship of *Nursing in a Multi-Ethnic NHS* (PSI, 1995) and *Changing Ethnic Identities* (PSI, 1994).

TARIQ MODOOD is Professor of Sociology, Politics and Public Policy at the University of Bristol. He was formerly Programme Director of PSI's Ethnic Equality and Diversity group, and his previous publications include principal authorship of the highly acclaimed *Ethnic Minorities in Britain: Diversity and Disadvantage* (PSI, 1997).

SATNAM VIRDEE is a Lecturer in Sociology in the Department of Government at the University of Strathclyde. He was previously Senior Fellow at the Policy Studies Institute. His main publications include *Racial Violence and Harassment* (PSI, 1995) and (as co-author) *Ethnic Minorities in Britain* (PSI, 1997).

Ethnic Minority Families

Sharon Beishon
Tariq Modood
Satnam Virdee

POLICY STUDIES INSTITUTE

UNIVERSITY OF WESTMINSTER

PSI is a wholly owned subsidiary of the University of Westminster

A CIP catalogue record of this book is available from the British Library.

ISBN 0 85374 746 6
PSI Report No. 857

Typeset by PCS Mapping & DTP, Newcastle upon Tyne
Printed in Great Britain by Page Bros, Norwich

Policy Studies Institute is one of Europe's leading research organisations undertaking studies of economic, industrial and social policy and the workings of political institutions. The Institute is a registered charity and is not associated with any political party, pressure group or commercial interest.

For further information contact
Policy Studies Institute, 100 Park Village East, London NW1 3SR
Tel: 0171 468 0468 Fax: 0171 388 0914 Email: pubs@psi.org.uk

Contents

Acknowledgements

This project was made possible by a grant from the Joseph Rowntree Foundation, for which we are grateful.

The project was assisted by an Advisory Group, to whom we are also grateful. The Advisory Group was initially chaired by Barbara Ballard, and then for most of the length of the project by Susan Taylor. We are particularly grateful for the comments we received from members of the Group on preliminary analyses and on drafts of this report. Particular thanks are due to our former PSI colleague, Professor Richard Berthoud, who was a member of the research team until his departure from PSI at an early stage in the project. His work on the Fourth National Survey of Ethnic Minorities and his contribution to the research design were important parts of the foundation on which this project was built.

The full Advisory Group was as follows:

Barbara Ballard (Joseph Rowntree Foundation)
Susan Taylor (Joseph Rowntree Foundation)
Dr Ravinder Barn (University of London)
Professor Richard Berthoud (University of Essex)
Dr Geoff Dench (Institute of Community Studies)
Lynthia Grant (Moyenda Project)
Professor Susan McRae (Oxford Brookes University)
Anne Mercer (Department of Health)
Pamela Smith (Commission for Racial Equality)
Professor David Quinton (University of Bristol)

We would also like to thank Dr Maggie Studholme, University of Bristol, for her editorial and drafting assistance.

Our final thanks are to those who helped us conduct the interviews, and, of course, to those who gave us interviews.

Summary

Ethnic minority families represent a diversity: they differ in significant ways from the White population and from each other. Underneath the statistical differences are differences in attitudes and norms.

- The idea of a family among Pakistani and Bangladeshi respondents included a continuing preference for multi-generational households, often with income held jointly and managed by the eldest male, and married women not in paid employment outside the home. While expected to prevail as a custom, it is envisaged that in future those getting married will have some say in the choice of spouse.

- African Asians and Indians practised a 'negotiated' form of arranged marriage, in which parents and the young people both have a say, and believed in the importance of marriage, preferably for life. On attitudes to marriage and bringing up children within marriage there could therefore be said to be a shared Asian view. However, on issues such as women having paid employment outside the home and inter-marriage, African Asian and Indian views are closer to African-Caribbeans and Whites than other Asians.

- African-Caribbeans were likely to emphasise an individualism: independence and physical and emotional 'space' were necessary for individual maturity and the value of commitments is believed to be based on the quality of relationships, not custom, duty or a marriage certificate. Marriage and joint parenting were valued as an ideal by the majority of respondents, including unmarried lone parents.

- Many of the ethnic minority respondents in this study thought their families were very different from those of the White population (in some cases this made them disfavour mixed relationships). The most cited difference was a negative perception. White parents were thought to lack a commitment to parenting, with the result that White children were thought to be indisciplined and lacking in respect for their parents and elders.

- A multicultural approach has, therefore, to support a diversity in partnering and parenting. It has to support lifestyles which emphasise the importance of multi-generational households, lifeterm marriages and two-parent households, as well as supporting lifestyles where these are not desired or thought feasible.

Chapter 1

Diversity

Ethnic minority families are a genuine diversity; there are important points of contrast between them and the White majority, as well as between different minority groups. This diversity is sometimes, implicitly or explicitly, taken to be problematic, as if approximation to the behaviour of the White British is morally worthy or a sign of progress, and variation from that behaviour is deviant. Our starting point is the opposite, namely that there is nothing inherently worrying about diversity as long as members of minority communities find satisfaction in the lifestyles and family formations that they find themselves in. Social policy will increasingly have to be alive to this diversity. This study is, therefore, concerned not with identifying problematic behaviour but in providing some insight into the lived experience behind the statistics that we are becoming familiar with, and in illuminating the norms and attitudes that shape ethnic minority family formations, and the ways they are changing. As with any group of people, including the White population, there will be internal differences, and there will be concerns and worry about inertia and change. We focus on these in the belief that they are a much better indication of what the issues are than the application of majoritarian norms.

There are now considerable statistical data about Asian and Black households and families. The Fourth National Survey of Ethnic Minorities is a key source for identifying the diverse family formations in Britain, and the one we rely on. Detailed analysis of this data set is to be found in Modood et al. (1997). Chapters 2 and 9 of that study, on households and ethnic identity respectively, are an essential companion to the present book. The present study has to be seen in the context of the statistical findings of the Fourth Survey. We do not have the space to repeat those findings here, but, for the convenience of the reader, the key findings, which provide the statistical base on which the present study is built, are presented in Appendix A.

PURPOSE OF THIS STUDY

It is clear from the statistical data that the Caribbean and Asian groups are different from the White British population in some significant respects. Moreover, these differences are likely to be relevant to a range of social and economic debates and policies; for example, policies to do with the extent of poverty and how best to assist poor households. It is equally clear that the statistics do not suggest that the ethnic minorities differ from the White majority in the same way. The ways in which the Caribbeans differ from the majority are radically different from the ways in which, say, the Bangladeshis differ from the majority – and indeed these minorities differ more from each other than they do from Whites. On the other hand, these 'differences' are not static but subject to change, though some trends and continuities are statistically discernible.

Yet, to properly appreciate what is changing and likely to carry on changing, and in what direction, we need to go beyond the statistics. We need to have a sense of what people take their circumstances to be, what are their reasons for change, what aspects of their practices and norms they take to be negotiable, what changes they will resist and so on. In short, we need to have a feel for the lived experience, to identify the values that are guiding groups of individuals and the attitudinal changes that may be taking place.

There are aspects of the statistical findings – short-term relationships, inter-racial partnerings, lone parenthood, large families, full-time motherhood and homemaking, arranged marriages and so on – that worry some people. They are the object of media and political debate and stereotyping even when the discussion is about British society in general and there is no explicit reference to race and ethnicity. They can be particularly hostile when an ethnic minority group is the object of debate. This can be true even when the discussion is conducted by members of the minority group in question (for examples, see Song and Edwards, 1996).

Statistics record behaviours; they do not by themselves tell us whether people want to live one way or another, or why people live the way they do. The best way forward is to explore what the 'problematic' circumstances mean for the people whose circumstances they are. In this way we may gain some understanding of whether people whose lives look 'deviant' from the outside are living in ways that they prefer or find satisfying, or are happy with the compromises that they may be making. We hope, thereby, to avoid the pathologising of ethnic minority families and practices by bringing out the concerns of ethnic minority people themselves, to give some space to the values and debates within ethnic minority families and relationships.

This, then, is our immediate purpose. If it is successful, we will have introduced the facts and values of diverse relationships into the purview of the policy domain. Families are a field where policy and law are, and perhaps must be, guided by a moral perspective, by an idea of what are more or less desirable ways of living. Yet this study emphasises the value diversity that is to be found and which should be incorporated into policy perspectives. There is perhaps an inevitable tension here between the commitment to diversity and the commitment to a wider ethical perspective. We do not offer any answers on this matter here, but hope to contribute towards raising awareness that these issues are there, that they are difficult and that they are part of a multicultural society. Our starting point is that all communities offer something positive to their members and, by extension of our common humanity, to others outside the community. The wider society, therefore, at any one time may have something to learn from the minority, as well as the other way round.

Finally, we hope that our sympathetic presentation of the viewpoints of diverse groups may possibly lead to some caution about generalisations to the effect that all the important contemporary trends are pointing in the same direction, that the variety to be witnessed amounts to a 'relationship revolution' (Dormor, 1992), that we have moved from one epoch of family-life to another (Giddens, 1992), or that there is a singular trend towards greater individualism that most people are happy with (McRae, 1997: 387; Coote, Harman and Hewitt, 1998). If we are able to suggest that contemporary societies are more complex than these generalisations suggest, we will have contributed to getting ethnic minorities taken more seriously in the sociological literature than they have been to date.

METHODS

The Fourth National Survey of Ethnic Minorities, as well as our earlier qualitative work (Modood, Beishon and Virdee, 1994), made it clear that the ethnic minority families there studied fell into three groupings:

- Caribbean families

- Indian and African Asian families

- Pakistani and Bangladeshi families.

We selected a sample of Fourth Survey households from each of these groupings to revisit for a further in-depth interview. We selected a range of households within each grouping but tried to ensure that those households that were particularly strongly associated with a grouping were well represented in the relevant sample. There was, however, no attempt to make these samples representative of the populations they were drawn from. We were not trying to replicate our quantitative analyses but to probe behind the statistics into the lived experience, values and attitudes that were part of the processes that created the various patterns of family life. In some households, an interview with a second member of the household was taken in order to gain a second perspective.

Some White family members were also interviewed. There was no intention to offer a separate case study of White families, as there is no lack of such detailed studies. White interviewees were selected simply to offer some comparison with ethnic minority respondents and these data are drawn upon in the comparative chapter, Chapter 5.

BREAKDOWN OF RESPONDENTS

A breakdown of respondents is offered opposite, and some further details are offered in subsequent chapters. This is simply so that the reader is aware of the key characteristics of the people whose opinions are being presented. These breakdowns and the use of numbers in the presentation in the substantive chapters are simply to inform about the respondents, not to offer quantitative analyses.

Table 1.1 Interviews

	African-Caribbean	Indian & East African	Pakistani & Bangladeshi	White
Women	18	13	12	14
Men	6	7	12	7
Total	24	20	24	21

Table 1.2 Family type

	African-Caribbean	Indian & East African	Pakistani & Bangladeshi	White
Single	3	2	4	1
Single Parent	5			6
Married/co-habiting	10	10	10	10
Multi-generation	1	4	5	

The interviews took place, by prior appointment, in the homes of the interviewees and lasted about one to two hours. They took place in various parts of London and were undertaken by experienced and trained depth-interviewers, in nearly all cases women, who were deliberately ethnically-matched with the interviewees. In this way we aimed to provide an appropriate atmosphere in which interviewees were comfortable about talking about very personal and private matters with a person who they had reason to believe would understand and sympathise with their point of view, and in a language they were comfortable with (most of the interviews with the South Asians were conducted in whole or in part in an Asian language).[*] The interviews were tape-recorded and transcribed (after translation, if appropriate) in full. They were subject to formal content analysis based on grids. The analyses are presented in the subsequent chapters

---

[*] It has to be said that while these arrangements worked well in many ways, it did sometimes mean that some Asians relied on the implicit cultural understanding of the interviewer in order not to have to spell things out, using phrases such as 'You know what I mean...', 'you know what it is like amongst our people', etc. We trained our interviewers to probe behind such answers, but there was a limit to how much probing could be attempted, especially on sensitive matters.

with minimal comment from the researchers and, within the limits of space, maximum use of respondents' own words.

Information was collected on:

- *Household:* who lives in the household, their relationship to each other, desire/reluctance for other family within the household.

- *Relationships:* information about present and past personal relationships, attitudes towards marriage and divorce.

- *Children:* family size, childcare, education, contact with family outside of household.

- *Economy:* work and income, economic relationships with other households, attitudes towards working women.

- *Identity:* ethnic, cultural and religious identity, perceptions of group distinctiveness, attitudes towards exogamy.

- *Support:* help given and received within the family, expectations of family support.

- *Family:* relationship with parents and siblings, expectations of role of family.

The interviews were semi-structured, giving freedom to the interviewer to pursue some topics conversationally as the context allowed. Not all topics were equally covered in all interviews and some group differences were evident. For example, Muslims had much more to say about the relevance of religion, while the Caribbeans had a lot to say about the respective pros and cons of cohabitation compared to marriage. It would be fair to say that we found that the Caribbean interviewees were both more willing and able to discuss the topics of this study, and gave longer answers than the Asians. The Asians often thought that the answers to some questions were obvious and did not require elaboration; on some matters, especially questions about pre-marital relationships, the interviewers had to exercise great skill, circumlocution or brevity in order to not give offence.

The findings of the in-depth interviews are reported in the next three chapters, taking one ethnic minority grouping at a time. The fifth chapter compares these findings, and the concluding chapter stresses the theme of taking diversity seriously, arguing that, despite talk about a 'relationship revolution', it is wrong to assume that partnering and parenting in Britain reflect a singular set of trends.

Chapter 2

African-Caribbean Families

We interviewed 24 individuals from 19 households. In five households we spoke to more than one person. This was sometimes the initial respondent's partner and sometimes a child aged over 16.

Table 2.1 Family forms

	Single (no children)	*Single Parent Div/Sep/ Widow*	*Single Parent (never married)*	*Married/ Cohab 2 + years*
Men	1	1	0	4 (married)
Women	2	4*	6	5 (married) 1 (cohab)

- The gender imbalance was due to a decision to focus on single parents.

- All six men were African-Caribbean, and two had children from a previous relationship, living outside their household, as well as children from their current relationship.

- One woman (*) lived in a three generation household with her children and grandchild. Another had a child from a previous relationship but not living with her.

- Fourteen women were African-Caribbean; one was mixed Black-African and African-Caribbean, one was mixed African-Caribbean and White British, and two were White women married to African-Caribbean partners. We interviewed the White women because we had also spoken to their husbands, giving us a fuller picture of these families and reflecting the fact that the Caribbean group is not a neatly bounded one.

• Households were typically made up of a couple or single parent and their child or children. We had a single example of grown-up siblings living in the same household which was not the parental home.

RELATIONSHIPS

Current relationships

Three of the married men were married to White British women. Three of the women were currently in mixed relationships with White British men and two had previously been in mixed relationships: one with a Black-African man, and another with a White British man.

Eleven of the 14 respondents who were not married or living as married (nine female single parents and two grown-up children of respondents, one female and one male) were not in a current relationship. This number seems high and it may have been possible that some respondents preferred not to mention current relationships. Only three of the female single parents were currently in relationships and in only one case was this with the father of one of her children.

Of the nine currently married, all had lived with their partner before marriage. One couple had been living together for over nine years and expected to marry in the future.

Past relationships

Only two respondents claimed never to have had a relationship, and three respondents currently in long-standing marriages had never had any other relationship. Three respondents gave no indication of previous relationships. Three had previously been married, but had not lived with their partner first. Three never-married female single parents had experience of previous relationships but had not cohabited. Nine had previously cohabited with a partner. For three, this was a prelude to marriage.

Attitudes towards marriage and cohabitation

Most respondents expressed positive feelings about marriage and often saw cohabitation as a pragmatic first step towards it.

Cohabitation as a prelude to marriage

Most of our respondents, regardless of their own status, felt very positively about marriage. It was seen as a forward step, a progression in a relationship.

> *No, it [discussions about marriage] didn't come up before we were living together. It came up after we were living together. Time progressed and the relationship progressed. It [marriage] sort of became like the next step of what we should do...*

Marriage means more than living with someone

Most felt marriage was more important than living with someone. Some felt this was associated with religious belief in the sanctity of marriage, although only two described themselves as currently practising their religion.

> *I believe in the institution of marriage. If I'm good enough for you to live with, I'm good enough for you to marry.*

> *Ultimately, I'd like to be married but ... It's like I'd have to live with him a little while before I start the marriage business.*

> *... We are from very staunch Jamaican families, and in those days it was a natural progression. If you went to live with somebody, her mother would expect you to marry her daughter. There was no question of anything else ... [in] the Pentecostal Church, if you are courting a girl from church, you are expected to marry her.*

Cohabitation and marriage are the same

A few respondents felt there was little difference between marriage and cohabitation. Marriage was *'just a piece of paper'*.

Marriage is not important at all

A very small number of respondents felt negatively about marriage or that it was really unimportant, although this included one person who was currently married.

The benefits for the children

Many respondents expressed mixed and contradictory feelings about whether it was important to be married before having children. In general, they felt that commitment between two people was the most important thing. About half the respondents felt that marriage before children was not important. They saw little if any difference between marriage and cohabitation.

> *What's so different about people who are married or people who are not married when they have children? I think they're all the same, they've just a different title.*

> *What is marriage, it's just a piece of paper isn't it? It just legitimates everything ... You might say your son's a bastard and your daughter's a bastard but at the end of the day that piece of paper legitimates it. That's all it does and if the marriage is shit, then what's the point...?*

Being married brings more security

The other half of the respondents felt that it was important to be married before having children, usually because marriage was more secure. Some also felt that marriage implied a stronger relationship than cohabitation and was therefore less likely to break down.

> *... a lot of people if they have children before they are married ... the relationship is not that strong and it can be easily broken up, whereas if you are married ... then it's probably a little bit harder for it to break up.*

> *... it would be wonderful if they were married because then the child knows [the father], you know the child can easily get the father's name, the identity. [The child] feels the security that's coming from that married relationship. If two people are living together and the relationship is solid and they have children, that's fine. Where it is just a play around relationship that's a pity because it's usually in those relationships that it [the child] was never planned. The intentions weren't there to have children, but the children came along. So it would be better if they were married. Very often when they are married it's [children] something they have planned and wanted ... but that can also go for a committed relationship as well.*

Single parenthood is not ideal

Most respondents, even those with experience of single parenting, did not feel it was an ideal environment in which to raise children. They believed that two parents were essential to the emotional growth, development and general wellbeing of children.

> *... The ideal is that every home should have a mummy and a daddy ... but we're not living in an ideal world and things don't always work out that way. I mean through no fault of anybody's. Things happen. I think children are more stable, I really do, I think it does help their stability when they have two parents. I really do believe that because [I] must say I do feel they miss out on one [if one parent is absent]. It doesn't matter how you look at it. I do feel it makes a difference and I do feel they miss out on something. I think maybe it's a security thing. It's a confidence thing ... Confidence has a lot to do with it. I think that when they grow up on their own they tend not to be so confident, self-assured ...*

One respondent felt single parenting to be a particular problem for the African-Caribbean community.

> *... I think that looking at society and looking at what's happening with young, unmarried, especially Afro-Caribbean and their children. The girls are having babies for this man or that man and the children don't know if they are coming or going and don't know their fathers. I think that's wrong and I don't think it's fair to the children. And we are seeing the problems in schools, the way children behave and they haven't got any role model to look up to. Dad's not there. Who is my dad? ... Mum's struggling to provide for them and they might have all the gear and anything else, but they don't have any role models. I do think they should really have a marriage mate before they have children. At least make some firm commitment because this don't help the children.*

Commitment is the important thing

The majority of respondents felt that relationships were about the level of commitment between two individuals, regardless of whether that relationship was legally recognised. They felt that level of commitment to the children could be achieved almost regardless of commitment between parents. Even so, they believed that marriage gave stability to a relationship, and therefore had a greater chance of success than cohabitation. When children were involved, marriage could provide them with security, emotional benefits, inner confidence, and positive role models, that might be lacking if their parents cohabited.

Attitudes towards divorce

More than two thirds of respondents felt that divorce was permissible, especially if the couple were very unhappy together and could not get on.

> *... I believe that anything that goes wrong in a relationship, everybody should have it in them to forgive that person, but if some matters are unresolvable, if two people really cannot get on, and they have tried to work at it, and they have done all that they can to repair it, or put it back together, or build it up and strengthen it and it's unresolvable, then rather than living in strife and in distress and in hatred towards one another, then it's best to go separate ways.*

Although a few felt that divorce was permissible only in very extreme circumstances such as physical cruelty, most suggested that it was preferable to staying in an unhappy relationship, when the effect on children might be worse.

> *... if you have children and the children are seeing you two unhappy I think rather than having your children subject to that sort of thing, subjecting your children to [emotional] abuse. That's how I see it. I really wouldn't want my children being subjected to that sort of abuse because then we as a couple will be giving those kids the impression that that's what marriage is all about ... So for their sakes as much as yours, I think it's best to make a clean break.*

Family pressure?

Most respondents with experience of cohabitation – whether now or in the past – felt that their families were less concerned about the legal status of a relationship than about whether they were happy. Families were more likely to be upset at pregnancy outside of a marriage or cohabitation or at the possibility of divorce for a married couple.

... My mum was very upset, even to this day. She won't admit to a lot of people that I'm divorced. She don't want me to talk about it. A lot of people still think I'm married ... She's got this thing about he didn't beat me so it couldn't have been that bad.

GENDER DIFFERENCES

Expectations of marriage

Overwhelmingly, respondents believed that there were gender differences in expectations about marriage. In general, women were perceived to gain security and a particular kind of identity from marriage. It was considered to signify increased commitment from male partners, and it gave them increased social status amongst their friends and family. For men, marriage was considered to bring additional responsibility.

> *I believe it [marriage] is not important to me. I've been doing a survey of men in my head, and if you ask 100 men do they really want to get married, 80 of them would say no, [but they do] because of peer pressure from their friends and families to be seen as normal. With women it is different. That [marriage] is the fantasy for women. You are a fully grown woman if you are married and have kids. If you are not, there is something wrong with you.*

Another female respondent felt that men were more concerned with their commitment on a daily basis rather than isolated public declarations. Both men and women were more likely to feel that marriage for men was mainly important in functional terms, i.e. getting regular meals, having their washing done and their children looked after, and regular sex.

> *I think men are quite happy to be in a stable relationship but I think they have more of the attitude that it should be enough that they come home every day and are not off, out, so why do you need marriage to prove anything else ... [For women] it [marriage] is more important in terms of women looking for commitment and they think if they [men] want to marry you, it must mean that they love you more or whatever, but even that attitude is changing now. I think there is a general sense of opinion where that more and more couples just live together.*

One male respondent felt marriage was just as important for men because of the power it gave them over women and children.

> *It gives them [men] a sense of territory. I think even that children given a man's surname says something about how important it is for them to know or belong.*

Religion is more important than gender

A few respondents felt it was not gender, but religion, that was the decisive factor, with marriage being more important to the religious than the non-religious.

Domestic responsibilities

Most of our respondents – among whom were 14 single parents – were in paid employment, full or part-time.

Domestic labour was predominantly carried out by women, usually wives and mothers, regardless of their commitments outside of the home. Only one male single parent said that he did his own housework. Another man suggested that domestic labour was shared between the couple, while another said he did the cooking and his wife did the rest. Older children were often expected to keep their own belongings and rooms tidy. Communal areas were also sometimes allocated to children to clean and tidy.

INTER-GENERATIONAL RELATIONSHIPS

Adult children on living with parents

The Fourth Survey found that a third of Caribbean elders lived with an adult child, but our respondents, overwhelmingly, did not want either parents or parents-in-law living with them. One respondent felt it was a very old-fashioned Caribbean model that had become outdated and superseded in the UK.

Most respondents initially focused on the issue of space to explain why they did not want to live in a multi-generational household. A small number suggested that if they occupied a large enough property to accommodate additional family members then this might be a possibility. Money was also a key factor, with respondents feeling unable to financially support any others within the household. For most, however, there was little underlying desire to live in very close contact with parents – especially once they had established their own home and family.

> *No, because everyone's got their own life to lead. I think you get to a certain age when you need to go your own way. I think you should keep in touch with each other obviously, but I think you need your own space.*

Respondents used the idea of 'space' not only as a physical dimension, but also to describe a process of emotional distancing or separation. They felt that breaking ties with home and parents was a positive way of building life and emotional skills.

> *... I think after a while they should find their own space and also I think it helps them to grow up and see what life is all about. Let's face it, if they're living at home all the time they're gonna think things are easy. They're not gonna take responsibility for their adult life are they? It's good that the child should move out at some point.*

Respondents believed that parents and adult children had very different needs – difficult, if not impossible, to accommodate within a single household. Some felt that living with parents meant they would always be cast in the role of the 'child', regardless of age.

> *... You want different things and you don't want to encroach other people. You need to give that person breathing space to grow. If you're there, 24/7 it would be suffocating.*[*]

For young adults still living at home, there was something central to the process of growing-up and becoming a fully fledged adult that involved not only leaving home but not returning. Few saw the possibility of benefits and additional support that elders might give to grown-up children and grandchildren (contrary to the views of the respondents of another study (Hylton 1997: 14–15)).

---

* 24/7 is a term commonly used amongst urban youngsters. It has been popularised through African-American music and means 'all the time', i.e. 24 hours a day, seven days a week.

Respondents expressed similar feelings about living with siblings, although a minority felt it might work if the relationship between them was good. Having siblings local enough to give and receive support was generally popular, so long as they were far enough away to allow each their privacy.

Parents on living with adult children

If adult children did not want to live with their parents, neither did parents express much desire to live with their adult children. Most felt that this would entail some loss of independence and status, and might lead to them becoming a burden upon their children. As one father suggested:

> *Well, because I suppose independence really ... I would not like to cramp their style, it would be unfair on them... I think if I lived with my son and daughter and I saw something I would really have to say it, and that could cause a lot of trouble.*

Another suggested that

> *I wouldn't want to saddle my daughter with me in the future if I'm getting on [old age]. I want her to have her own life and do what she wants to do. Even if she wanted to, I don't think I would want that. No.*

> *... I don't want to be dependent upon anybody. I hope to God, I pray to God all my faculties will be there and I'm not an old woman that I become so dependent upon somebody else. I want to be agile. I want to be up and down all the time, so that I'd not become a burden to my children, they should be free to live their own life, not think about me.*

Ill health or destitution were among the few acceptable 'excuses' parents cited for living with grown-up children:

> *It would depend on the circumstances. If the parents are destitute – White people tend to put the old in a home – black people would look after their own. We're too proud. I'd have no qualms about that.*

Only one respondent out of 24 – a single parent – wanted her parent to live with her. She felt that having a grandparent within the household offered the advantage of shared child care and domestic labour.

A sense of responsibility

In spite of a general lack of desire to live with parents, some respondents felt quite strongly that children owe their parents a debt which can be repaid in old age. Both parents and adult children felt it was better to live near one another, which was seen as the best of both worlds. Parents would be near enough to offer help and support when needed but far enough away for their children to have their own privacy.

> *... I'm of the school where parents spend x amount of years raising you and [when grown-up] it's about time you go out, and if anything you are helping them and they are not helping you. I think it is a two-way street between parents and children. So no. I think you should be able to lead an independent life. There is an exception where you can still live with your parents but even though you're living in your parents' house you're not still expecting your parents to do all the things that they used to do when you were growing up. So instead of them constantly helping you, you're actually giving something back to them.*

> *Well, for the obvious benefits that the children will have grandparents close ... You will be able to help your parents out when they need it. As they get older they generally need more help and if necessary then can help you out if you need it...*

Contact with family outside the household

About a third of the respondents were happy with the amount and type of contact they had with their own parents. Some respondents with living parents would have liked to have more contact, but were constrained by finance or time to do so – especially if their parents lived overseas.

A significant number of respondents had little if any contact with their own fathers, though this was not always out of choice. Some respondents simply did not know the whereabouts of their fathers.

Family overseas

All African-Caribbean respondents had family members living overseas, usually in the Caribbean, North America or Canada and sometimes in two of these three locations. In most cases these were close family members such as parents or siblings. All respondents were in contact with some family members living abroad. Many had been to visit them or had hosted such visits within the previous five years. Nearly all wanted more face to face contact but were financially constrained.

Gender roles in the family

Roles are interchangeable

For about half of the respondents, from a variety of family types (including single parents), the roles played by mothers and fathers were flexible and interchangeable. They did not expect fathers to fulfil any special duties or that fathers had any special responsibilities. At least one respondent said that fathers were simply not important. Indeed, mothers were seen as taking responsibility for all of the family's needs. Grandparents were an additional extra who were useful when available, but certainly not essential to the running of a home or the development of children.

Roles are fixed

A significant proportion of respondents, again from a variety of family types (including some single parents), described how their family still operates traditional roles with the mother as carer and nurturer and the father as protector and provider.

> *I think the mother's the stabiliser. I think the mother is someone you should always be able to go to and talk to. She's the one who puts the plaster on the knee, gives you the cuddle and tells you that you're really special and really wonderful, 'cause Daddy's always at work and Mummy's always there, 24 hours a day to take care of you. The father I think is supposedly the person that goes out there and gets the money and provides a roof over your heads. He's there on Saturdays and Sunday afternoons to go and kick a ball about and do all those things.*

Grandparents' roles

Grandparents were expected to take on a specific role related to the emotional or moral development of the child. Grandparents were expected to 'spoil' children and give them additional time, affection and goods that parents could not afford.

> ... *a grandparent comes round with presents and a bag of sweets. Takes you out and buys you nice things ... Their role is to love you lots and spoil you.*

Grandparents were also an important link with the past and family history.

> ... *For Roxanne, she has her great grandmother, which is my mum's mum, over here and she was fascinated and would just sit down there and let grandmother talk about what mummy used to do when she was younger, and hear all about Jamaica, so I think it also brings in the heritage, the background, where you coming from ... which helps make you who you are and who you are going to be in the future.*

CHILDREN

Time spent with children

Some parents with children living with them wanted to spend more time with them. Of these parents, two mothers and one father suggested it was the pressure of work that meant they did not have as much time as they would have liked to spend with their children. Another (who did live with his children) had re-organised his work in order to spend more time with his children:

> ... *When the first two were coming along [growing up] we moved. We were building a home, buying things and I used to do a lot of extra hours at the Post Office to earn money to take care of them. I didn't seem to have sufficient time [with them and for them], for a weekend isn't sufficient ... I didn't have sufficient time at night to sit down and chat with them ... [One night] I came in about half past ten ... and I thought they [the children] were asleep ... when*

[one] came down with this books and said 'Dad I want your help ... I've got something here I can't seem to understand'. He was going to secondary school at the time ... so the two of us sat down. I thought this wasn't right, so I changed my time of duty to 7pm and was home every night by 8 o'clock which meant that any problems they had, I was there to help them.

Most female single parents suggested their child/children had little if any contact with their fathers, and only one single parent was satisfied with the amount of contact her child had with its father. Two fathers whose children did not live with them felt they would have liked more contact.

Some parents with children in the household were satisfied with the amount of time they spent with them. Three of these were in paid employment, including one in full-time work. Two others were looking after children full-time and one was a student whose timetable allowed her to study around the demands of her family.

Full-time childcare as a positive choice

Parents who were caring for their children full-time saw this as a positive alternative to paid work.

At the moment I spend a hundred per cent [of my time] with my son ... I want a lot for him and because I didn't have this privilege with my first child I'm not going to miss out on the second time around. So I'm quite prepared to put my career, or whatever, on hold for a short time to give him what he needs as a start.

Children and education

Only a third of respondents with children were satisfied with their children's education and schooling. Even these parents – one of whom sent their child to a private school – had reservations and did not feel the current curriculum was broad enough. In fact, most parents wanted to add to their child's school curriculum. They wanted to include Black history and culture or lessons that would help to shape a positive identity. Some parents wanted lessons that would build confidence and self-respect. A smaller number wanted practical lessons on how to deal with prejudice and racism or how to beat the system and 'act White'. A few parents felt their children should learn about other cultures, nationalities or religions.

We are somebody too

> ... I do feel that Black History is a very important part for Black children, because I think a lot grow up still thinking we've got no history and there's no role model for us when it's not really so.

> ...children are still being taught in the frame of mind where White is superior, and that's what English history teaches you. White is superior and White is right... I feel that every child should be taught that English people did this, the Indians did this, the Black man did this, the Chinese man did this. Then they will know that, as like their own people, our people are somebody too. They're not just second class citizens, here to do whatever. We are somebody too.

Teach the Whites not to be racist

One parent, a father of a mixed-ethnicity child, felt the emphasis should not be on adding or including something for children of mixed heritage but rather for those children and adults with prejudiced views forcing mixed-ethnicity children to take on exclusively Black or White identity.

> ... my daughter shouldn't have to be taught where she comes from. The people who make or create the problem and make trouble should be taught.

Another father also felt the focus should be on White staff and pupils:

> They should be taught Black culture so that the White people don't come and rub your boy's head and say 'your hair needs combing' or say 'you're so lucky you don't need to wash your hair'. We have to wash our hair everyday! Or they see you greasing your skin and they ask stupid questions. Then [you get] the myth about Black people are the descendants of monkeys and that you come out of the trees. Let them know that Black people are a proud people ...

Education is partly the parents' job

One parent felt there was not enough taught about religion and gender issues. Another felt that these additional lessons were not the job of teachers, but of parents:

> *... Generally I think it has to come from within the family. There are things you need to discuss about how to get on as a Black child, a Black person in this culture. I talk to my son and I say to him, we know you have to try harder than the next person to get on, and this is a fact of life. I think it is my duty to make him aware of that, and I say to him there is no such thing as fairness in this life ... you need to teach your children, don't give them the impression that there is equality out there, because that is a myth, there is not ...*

Learning to 'act White'

Some parents felt that lessons on how to deal with racism and prejudice should be included. They suggested a number of strategies, including learning how to act 'White', which focused on resolving disputes by verbal communication, being passive, and not actively resisting racist jibes and insults:

> *... make sure they are always in agreement with the White man, even though they don't agree, do you get me? Just to get on, even though you don't agree, you know you just sort of accept it ... just to be able to get through, even if you don't agree, but just to get through life.*

Cultural activities

In spite of their insistence on the importance of Black history and culture, most parents said their children did not take part in any cultural or religious activities outside school. Of those who did, all but one attended or took part in activities related to the church or religion. This included Sunday School, participation in religious playgroups, after-school church clubs or religious studies at home under parental instruction. In addition to a church-based Sunday School, one child attended a Black-run Saturday School which covered broad curriculum areas and included Black culture and history.

Mixed relationships

Six of the respondents were in mixed relationships, and nearly all respondents' families had relatives who were or had been in a mixed relationship. These were usually, but not exclusively, with White

British partners. Even so, more than a third of our respondents were unhappy with the idea of mixed relationships. Most of these people had never had a relationship outside of their own ethnic group. One respondent had a relationship with a Black African and another was herself of mixed Black-African and African-Caribbean heritage. However, even close family experience did not necessarily make respondents sympathetic towards, or happy about, such unions:

> ... *I don't want to sound hypocritical because I have a mixed race niece, my brother lives with a White lady. I don't like it, but I can accept it.*

In the Fourth Survey more than four out of five Caribbeans said that they would not mind a close relative marrying a White person. Amongst our respondents, views on mixed marriages were much more polarised. A substantial minority felt mixed partnerships could lead to loss of culture, confusion about identity for children; that it provided a bad role model for children; and that for some it amounted to little more than a technique for social climbing.

> ... *Personally I have a boy who is 14. He is very brainy and now goes to school in [the London borough of] Kingston, his last school was in Dulwich. He has never been to Brixton. I can see through no fault of his own, he is going White. He speaks White. The other day he came in with a Pamela Anderson poster, so my wife said to him that there are Black women, like Naomi Campbell, and she put them [posters] up on the wall. He was really vex [angry] and took them down. She confronted him about it and he said 'look Mum, if you can find a Black woman for me, I will go out with one, but I can't find one.' That really vex me ... In a nutshell, each to his own, but I am against it.*

> ... *some people think they are stepping up the ladder doing that [mixed relationship] and that is a problem for me, but if they have genuinely met someone they like and they just happen to be from a different culture, that's different.*

> *I don't mind the ones who go into that relationship because they like that person. They're not thinking, she's White, things are gonna happen for me, which a lot of these [people in] mixed relationships do.*

Respondents suggested that mixed-ethnicity children can end up feeling superior to their black peers. In addition, White mothers were considered unable to fully understand their child's experience of racism.

> ... *his daughter is now questioning why does she look different from the other children she goes to school with [in Ireland]. When I sent a photograph at Xmas of her cousins, she was so overjoyed, she said there are other people that look like her.*

Mixed relationships were perceived to be more prone to failure than other relationships.

> ... *I think there are extra disadvantages in a way, because it is diffi-cult enough being a couple [and] then to have quite a lot of cultural differences that can lead to a lot of additional problems ... there is more room for lack of communication because if somebody does not understand particularly where you are coming from, that gives you more scope for problems. I think they have definite disadvantages.*

The majority of respondents were not so pessimistic. About a third of respondents did not think that mixed relationships were an issue. They felt that race and culture were not as important as how two people treated each other, or that love was a lottery with little respect for colour or religion.

> *Love is colour blind. Love isn't racist ... As far as I'm concerned if I meet someone it doesn't matter where they're from and we care for each other and they treat me good and vice versa and we get on, that's fine by me ...*

There was yet another third of respondents who were actually positive about mixed relationships. All of these were either in a mixed relationship, usually with a White British partner, or had experience of one. They thought that mixed relationships broke barri-ers between people and so were good for individuals and society, and gave the children of such relationships a richer heritage than they otherwise would have. One respondent felt that a relationship with a White British person was more acceptable than with an African because of the practice of polygamy.

Despite this spread of views being different from the Fourth Survey findings, we found similar views expressed in some earlier in-depth interviews (Modood, Beishon and Virdee, 1994). It is quite clear that marriage with White people is a sensitive issue on which people may have mixed feelings.

Similarities and differences with other groups

African-Caribbeans are different from Whites

Most respondents felt their families to be both different from White British families and similar to other African-Caribbean families they knew. Many felt these differences stemmed from the behaviour of young people. White youngsters were perceived to have little respect for parents and other elders. Examples were given of White children and adolescents swearing at or around parents, or generally being cheeky and disobedient in public:

> *Yeah, we bring our kids up different, well there was a little boy about five years old came in here one day and he was playing with my last boy at the time and he said 'I swear in front of my mum and dad.' I said 'Well, you won't do it in here.'*

> *In the way that I bring up my children because I take an interest in what they are doing, they're not up and down all over the place all times of night. I'm more concerned about their manners and how they are towards adults, family. That they show adults respect that is due to them.*

White parents were considered to be lax in their parental duties, allowing children to play outside of the home unattended, giving them a succession of snacks rather than proper meals and encouraging insolence by ignoring it. Respondents generally felt that bad behaviour was the result of a lack of discipline and physical punishment. One respondent felt that this had changed over time, for older Whites shared more similarities with Black families than younger Whites did.

One respondent suggested that White families were closer to each other and had a more open style of communication between the generations, where anything could be discussed. It was this familiar-

27

ity that had bred contempt, and a breakdown in respect which led to bad behaviour.

A few respondents felt that, on the contrary, White families were more distant with each other, not having or wanting much contact with each other. They felt that Black communities were family oriented.

African-Caribbeans and Whites are alike

A few respondents felt they were similar to both White and African-Caribbean families. This was mainly because they felt there were little differences between families from each group.

Two respondents – both in mixed relationships – felt their families to be similar to White families but different from African-Caribbean families.

African-Caribbeans are different from Asians

About half of respondents felt that Asian families differed from their own, even where some could not pinpoint the exact nature of the difference. Most commonly, respondents suggested that religion was more important in Asian families than in African-Caribbean families. A few cited extended family structures or stricter discipline. Others suggested that Asian families were more insular or close-knit than African-Caribbean families. One male respondent (whose White wife was present while he was interviewed) highlighted Asian attitudes towards women:

> ... *Like the men make all the decisions, they are the head of the family as such and the women just basically do as they are told and that is certainly different from our family.*

African-Caribbeans and Asians have some things in common

Most of the remainder felt that their families were not very different from Asian families. One respondent suggested that all ethnic minorities in Britain faced the same pressures and difficulties due to their different cultural backgrounds. Another suggested that 'when you dig deep we are all the same'.

A few respondents felt unable to comment because they did not know enough about Asian families.

Religion is more important than culture

Two respondents, who were Seventh Day Adventists, felt that they had more in common with those who shared their religion, regardless of their ethnicity.

Chapter 3

African Asian and Indian Families

Thirteen women and seven men in 16 households were interviewed. In four of the 16 households, more than one person was interviewed. Eleven of the sample were of African Asian origin and nine were of Indian origin.

Family forms

- *Nuclear families:* four had more than three children; six had less than three.

- *Multi-generational families:* one nuclear family plus the son's wife and daughter, and three nuclear families plus the respondent's mother, father or both.

- Two single people.

RELATIONSHIPS

Respondents' experience of marriage was varied:

Table 3.1

	No
Arranged marriage	12
Love marriage	2
Single (never married)	6

None of the married respondents had been married more than once.

Attitudes to marriage

Almost all our respondents felt that marriage was extremely important. It was accepted as 'normal' behaviour, and something that one did when the time was right:

> ... *it comes down from history. It is a law laid down by the creator ... as He has created male and female He has laid down the laws of marriage and if you flout those laws then obviously you will suffer.*

Arranged marriages

On the whole, respondents whose marriages were 'arranged' were people who had migrated to Britain. If length of marriage is an indicator of its success, then these marriages were highly successful: all of them had been married for over 12 years and almost half of them for over 20 years. During the interviews, it became increasingly evident that understandings of what constituted an arranged marriage were highly fluid. We identified at least two distinct types of arranged marriage:

- *Non-negotiable:* where the respondent had no direct involvement in the process of selecting a partner at all.

- *Negotiable:* where there was a process of negotiation between the child getting married and their parents. A potential partner would be chosen by the parents and introduced to the child, and the child would come to a decision about whether the individual was suitable. If they were, the logistics of organising the marriage would be left to the parents.

Non-negotiated marriages

This was rare among our respondents, and restricted to people over the age of 45. In India, the late teens and early 20s was regarded as the key age to get married. According to one individual, '*you are educated by this time*'. One woman in her late 40s told us how she was married at 16:

> *I didn't even meet him or see his photo. I was just engaged. The first time I saw him was at the airport. I had faith in my father who arranged this.*

Another woman in her late 50s reported that

> *In those days they used to marry daughters early. They would not allow them to get too old. They married me at 15. If a girl gets too old then she starts to think for herself and she will not marry who her parents tell her to marry.*

Negotiated marriages

A male respondent in his early 50s reported how he had been introduced to his wife by his parents but was ultimately able to decide for himself whether he was going to marry her:

> *We saw each other three times ... I told my parents that I liked her.*

Similarly, a female respondent in her late 30s said how her husband and she

> *went out a few times and the next month everything was arranged.*

Regardless of the conditions under which marriages were arranged, caste appeared to be the critical sifting criterion by which they came to decide upon a suitable partner. Other important factors included the earnings prospects of an individual and the importance of fitting in with a particular culture.

Love marriages

The two respondents who did not have an arranged marriage described the process by which they got married. One was a 50-year-old woman who came to the UK from East Africa as a student. She told us how she ended up sharing a flat with an East African student who eventually became her husband:

> *... we got together because we came from the same school in Kenya ... that was my first introduction to him. We became friends and then we went out together and two years later we were married.*

This couple lived together for two years before announcing to their parents that they wished to get married. It was easier for them to develop a relationship because her parents were still in Kenya.

Another who had a 'love marriage' was a woman in her 30s, who had known her husband for five years before they were married.

You know when you go out with someone and sort of like them and care for them. You know that marriage is the right thing.

Changing attitudes to marriage

Single respondents

Most of our six single respondents (two men and four women), believed that although they would have an arranged marriage it would be very different from the kind experienced by their parents. At least two reported that they had been involved in relationships established by themselves. Another was currently in the process of 'breaking up' with her boyfriend.

One said:

Today, it [an arranged marriage] means getting introduced to people through your parents and other family and then having your own personal choice to make a decision ... it's not a forced decision.

One single respondent, however, described the institution of marriage as one of patriarchal domination and expressed great reservations.

I don't necessarily agree with marriage because I think you compromise too much of yourself ... especially women [who] tend to adapt their behaviour to suit their partners... I tend to neglect my friends and focus more on him and his friends. I make sure he gets fed and what not. Personally, I would prefer to be living with him than actually being married. I think the actual tie of being married is quite stressful. I don't think that marriages are for life ... people change ... By living together I have the option of getting out and it is less painful.

Another woman told how she was likely to have an arranged marriage but did not rule out what she termed a 'love marriage':

I might find someone myself ... someone I've met and I think my parents would accept this.

Marriage in the future

We also asked the 14 respondents who had children what sort of marriage their children were likely to have. About half felt uncertain about this, partly because their children were still very young, and partly because, as one parent said,

I can't say, times are different ... very different to mine. They've got more choice.

Even those who believed that their children would have an arranged marriage described an institution that had undergone a thorough overhaul from their times. One mother said that she would ensure that her daughter was educated before she got married. Then

I will introduce the child to the person and she can decide whether she wants to get married or not. I am not going to force her.

A minority of parents believed their children were unlikely to have an arranged marriage. One mother said that her children would not have an arranged marriage because

they are brought up in this country ... [they are] a different generation.

A father whose daughter was studying medicine suggested that she had moved out of her parents' class, and that they would therefore be unable to find her a suitable partner.

If she can manage it, it would be better if she found someone herself. That way they can get to know each other ... other things like the husband's job need to be considered.

Children and marriage

Respondents – particularly those with children of their own – believed strongly that children should not be born out of wedlock. Reasons for this included societal pressure and emotional and financial security:

- Societal Pressure

  Mainstream society still believe in the institution of marriage ... so it is not right.

- Emotional Security

  I personally would not want children before marriage because I think marriage is a form of security and children thrive better in a secure atmosphere.

- Financial Security

  They should be married before having children. They are secure then ... money wise, financially they [will] be looked after properly.

Single respondents articulated similar views. Only one respondent explicitly accepted the idea of having children before marriage.

Attitudes to divorce

Only about half our respondents said they were against divorce. These respondents represented marriage as a compromise, and divorce as bad for children. The other half believed that staying together could make a bad situation even worse:

Marriage is a compromise

> *... they shouldn't get divorced, they should always give and take. The marriage will last only if you accept that there are some defects in myself and some defects in my husband. You have to compromise and try to improve yourselves ... you have to give and take.*

Divorce is bad for the children

> *If they can help it, they shouldn't [divorce]. Even more so when there are children because one parent cannot bring up the child as well as two.*

> *I don't believe in divorce ... you need to keep together for the children. I think if you have divorce you don't have security.*

Staying together just makes things worse

> *Marriage is like a friendship and if you don't get on with your friend you say good-bye and part as good friends ... you only have one life and you should be happy... when two people are not getting along, I think a child realises ... and then it affects them more.*

Some thought it was more difficult for Indians to divorce due to cultural constraints, such as the pressure brought to bear by the community:

> *There's more of a pressure not to [divorce] in Indian families because of what everyone else is going to say ... including the family.*

GENDER ROLES

Paid work

About half of the respondents were in paid employment; a third were in full-time education; and the remainder looking after children or retired. Only one person was unemployed. About half of the households had two adults in paid employment, the remainder had one.

Four households sent money to a parent or sibling living abroad. Another four, whose families were now reunited, had previously sent money. This was interesting evidence of duties and responsibilities beyond the 'nuclear family' but could not be pursued further as respondents were not keen to speak about these matters.

Domestic responsibilities

The domestic division of labour was asymmetrical. Women were expected to cook, clean and ensure the smooth running of the house, whereas the role of men was minimal. Male respondents justified this in ways that suggested that their partner or mother had taken the lead in determining such a relationship:

> *I have never been expected to do anything in the kitchen. Maintenance is my responsibility. She wouldn't like me to cook.*

Women tended to accept this division of labour. One respondent said she was happy and that cooking and cleaning were 'a woman's job'. Another respondent articulated something similar by suggesting that

> *in Indian homes, it is always the woman who does it.*

On women going to work

On the whole, respondents felt strongly that women should go out to work, though men and women gave different reasons for this:

- Most women believed that a second wage earner was critical to the maintenance of a 'decent' standard of living.

- Some men believed that women wanted to work only '*to prevent them from getting bored*'.

A minority argued that the women's desire to seek paid work should not adversely impact on the children. This meant that women should not work while their children were young:

> *If they can work and look after the family, they should do that. If they have children, women should spend the first years with their children.*

> *I think once you have a family then the woman should not work because the child needs the mother quite a lot ... from our personal experience I would say that has helped my child.*

CHILDREN

Children and housework

Of those that had children, almost all said their children – whether boys or girls – helped with the housework. However, there was also a strongly held view that they should help only in so far as it did not impede their studies.

Most children undertook 'ordinary' leisure activities such as piano lessons, karate, roller-disco, football, movies, TV and video. Only two respondents reported that their children engaged in Indian cultural activities. These involved learning Indian folk dance for one child, and learning Gujarati at home for another.

Children and discipline

Respondents believed strongly that children should obey and respect older people:

> *the first thing you teach your child is to respect the elders.*

However, this was strongly tempered by the belief that children must also learn to think and develop their views independently of their parents:

> *... we give them liberty. But then we expect them to obey our family members and listen to what we have to say ... and ask us about their decisions. Sometimes there are differences over ideas but we always compromise.*

Children and school

Either both parents or the husband alone made decisions regarding the child's schooling. About half were happy with the relations and contact they had with their children's teachers, while the remainder would have preferred to have more contact and feedback regarding how each child was progressing.

Only three respondents felt that Indian children should learn more about their culture. Two of these had no children themselves.

> *I don't think we're taught about our culture enough. I think more should be taught about it and I think it should be taught by other young people because the message will get through.*

One parent said that

> *schools could teach more about our language ... the little one wants this and says he wants to go to classes.*

Another believed that

> *there should be more of an understanding of the restrictions that are placed on children by their parents... the way they socialise should be appreciated more.*

A minority mentioned the problem of racism in school, with one parent recommending that schools should

> *educate children about different 'races' and culture so that minority children don't encounter as much racial prejudice.*

Another (childless) respondent believed that by the time the current generation grew up,

> *.... I don't think there'll be as much racism. At the moment there are differences between the two cultures. As time goes on, our kids won't be stopped from going out like we were. They'll be able to do what they want just as their Black or White friends.*

ATTITUDES TOWARDS MULTI-GENERATIONAL HOUSEHOLDS

Tradition

Most respondents believed strongly that adult children should live with their parents, at least until they were married, after which they should set up home on their own. Most also believed, however, that married children should live close to their parents.

Respondents recognised the need to respect their children's independence and privacy, especially after marriage, but also when they are single adults:

> *Well the simple reason is that when grown-up children live with their parents they're still dependent on their parents and they don't get self-confidence and they don't know how to look after themselves in a better way. Also their outlook doesn't change because somebody else is doing their thinking for them.*

Respondents also stressed the importance of family responsibility, believing that children should live near their parents to look after them:

> *They should live near each other because it keeps the family going and the family is very important.*

Siblings

Some respondents believed that adult children should live together, in order that they might take care of their parents.

> *I think they should live together because they should look after their parents, although it doesn't happen so often.*

Change?

For a minority of respondents, the desire for independence was critical. A woman in her late 20s living on her own argued that

> *... once you're an adult, you are your own person ... it is more difficult having parents who are from India, and especially mine who are not that progressive really. There is a real clash between what they consider appropriate and what I consider appropriate.*

CONTACT WITH FAMILY MEMBERS OUTSIDE THE HOUSEHOLD

Family overseas

Respondents maintained regular contact with members of their family in many different countries including Canada, America, India, parts of Europe and East Africa. These relatives were usually parents and siblings and their families. Most kept in touch by phone and letter. Importantly, there was also an average of about one to two visits every two years to the homes of relatives, reciprocated by visits from relatives from abroad. In this way, wider family networks were maintained across national boundaries.

Family in the UK

Most respondents saw close relatives in the UK at least once a week. For some this was enough, for others it wasn't:

> *I would like to meet them more often but it is difficult in this country ... everyone has to go to work, my husband works ... no time to go and visit more than this ...*

ETHNIC, CULTURAL AND RELIGIOUS DIVERSITY

The importance of religion

About three quarters of our respondents were Hindus, one was Muslim and the remainder Sikhs.

Hindus

Most felt that their religion influenced the way they led their life, including what they ate and drank, as well as praying daily. Religion offered them and their children a moral code of living. One respondent summed this up:

> *I think religion keeps us on the right path.*

A small number felt that religion was not important. One respondent described how she had been brought up a Hindu but felt it could come to dominate your life in an adverse fashion:

> *You have to keep going to religious things and then you've got no time for anything else.*

Another respondent suggested that religion

> *will not be important in how I bring up my children.*

Sikhs

Most Sikhs expressed similar views. Some Sikhs, however, felt that the impact of their religion was negative, constraining the choices available to individuals. One respondent said

> *It puts certain restrictions on us ... eating food or being expected to say prayers. We shouldn't drink [alcohol] or smoke.*

This woman said that she obeyed some rules and rejected others. She drank alcohol and ate meat but did not smoke.

MIXED RELATIONSHIPS

Experience of mixed relationships

Although all our married respondents were married to members of their own religious and ethnic group, about half knew of close relatives (uncles, sisters and brothers) who had mixed marriages with a White person. These relationships had appeared to have had mixed results, some ending in divorce, others continuing successfully.

Attitudes to mixed relationships

On the whole, respondents were not opposed to marriage with a White partner, though they recognised that mixed relationships could be difficult.

One respondent's sister, who had married a German, reported that

> *we get on very well with him and his family and he gets on well with ours. There's no hassles at all really.*

Others said

> *it's up to the individual who they wish to live with ... as long as they are good to each other and their families ... I have no objections at all.*

> *I don't mind, each to their own. It's about choice. At the end of the day, the reasons why people have criticisms of it is because they are worried about where our culture is going to go if we start marrying with other 'races'. What are our parents going to say? But if individuals are happy then it is alright.*

Another respondent suggested children of mixed marriages were more likely to experience racism (from both communities). Another believed that cultural differences were so large that the marriage was unlikely to last:

> *in the long-run they [will] probably encounter some difficulties because no matter what anyone says there is a big cultural difference.*

However, this respondent, who was in her 40s, felt that her children would find it relatively easier to overcome such barriers.

Towards more open views about marriage

Single respondents tended to articulate views that were even more open, and reported actual experience of relations with members of other ethnic groups. Indeed, one Indian respondent replied that

> *all my partners have been White so it is not really an issue for me. I don't think there is anything wrong with it.*

A minority still felt that cultural difficulties might be overwhelming. One respondent argued that such mixed relationships go

> *wrong more often than not. It works out well in the beginning but there are then difficulties. There are two sides, too difficult ... you don't know the culture.*

Marriage to members of other ethno-religious groups

There appeared to be more antipathy towards marrying members of other ethnic minority groups than Whites. One respondent, who had not objected to their son or daughter marrying a White person, felt antagonistic towards the idea of their marrying someone of Caribbean origin. Another expressed antagonism towards Asian Muslims because of past historical experiences.

> *I'm a biased person as far as Pakistanis are concerned ... I've got a lot of Muslim friends and its nothing to do with their religion ... Its because I was brought up in India before independence. I have very strong feelings. I wouldn't like to be associated with them ...*

ATTITUDES TOWARDS OTHER ETHNIC GROUPS

Attitudes towards White British people

Respondents felt they were very different from White British People.

- They felt their families were bigger and more cohesive.
  it's a lot bigger, a lot more close knit. A bit more worried about

keeping up the family name, that's important. We keep in touch with close and distant relatives more.

- There were differences in how they related to children.

... we would not leave our children with baby sitters and go out for an evening. We'll take them with us or leave them with our mum or not go out at all. It's just the way we see life.

- Their dietary habits were different. They did not eat meat, drink alcohol, or smoke, partly influenced by their religion.
- They felt that religion was more important to them than to White people.

I see very few [White people] practising their religion and their social behaviour is different. They go out more whereas Indians stay more with the family.

- They felt that White people were more 'free'.

We don't have as much freedom as they have. We're behind the times in terms of restrictions we impose. For example, marrying people: it would be more acceptable for a White person to marry an Asian person than an Asian person to marry a White person.

This was because Asians are

... prejudiced against White people. Because of past histories ... ignorance and follow what they've been taught.

Changing attitudes?

Only one woman in her late 20s said she had more in common with Whites than Indians:

I don't speak my lingo very well. And... I don't live at home and I am not married. I suppose I don't have much in common with other Indians any more. I don't feel restricted by my culture or my religion... I find [White people] are more open-minded ... they don't have pre-judgements about things ... they don't just say what their parents have told them to say. I feel they are a lot more independent.

Attitudes towards other ethno-religious groups

Our respondents highlighted differences between themselves and both African Caribbeans and Asian Muslims.

Differences from Muslims

One respondent argued that Muslims

> *have a different way of living. We're less strict compared to Muslim families. Religion influences Muslim families a lot more than Sikh families.*

Differences from African-Caribbeans

Respondents suggested that

> *Caribbean people are more like White people. They don't have any restrictions. Marrying, education – parents don't have as much influence as Asian parents. Religion doesn't come up as much as for Asians. Therefore, its not as important.*

> *... their values in life are totally different to Indian values ... they don't believe in education being the key factor ... They also do not believe in their responsibilities in terms of their partner or family ... they are more selfish and I think that this is a major problem.*

Chapter 4

Pakistani and Bangladeshi Families

We interviewed ten Pakistanis from nine households and 14 Bangladeshis from ten households. Half were men and half were women. Although only two were born in the UK, it is likely that a larger number had arrived in the UK as children and had been educated and brought up largely in the UK. In the three households where two or more people were interviewed, the additional interviews were carried out with grown-up children and/or children-in-law living within the household.

MULTI-GENERATIONAL HOUSEHOLDS

Traditional living arrangements

Traditionally, the extended family tends to focus and build upon the husband's family. On marriage, daughters traditionally go to live with her husband, and sons bring their brides into their parents' homes. However, the process of migration, difficulty in gaining visas, the specification of British housing stock and the need to find work have all had an effect. Respondents suggested that living in an extended family is not as common in the UK as in Pakistan and Bangladesh.

Only a small minority of respondents were living in an extended family, usually with in-laws and siblings (although some were living with wider family members, such as cousins). Some others would have liked to have other family members (especially parents or parents-in-law) living within the household, including one already living in an extended household. One parent would have liked to have her child live with her.

Extended families are ideal

Most respondents felt that living as an extended family in a single household was ideal, fostering deep and meaningful relationships between family members, and ensuring that the family functioned as a mutually rewarding support system.

> ... *if when we get the son married off, if his wife comes and the son lives here with her, then it'll be very helpful to me. Today we're old, they'd look after us, sometimes cook and feed us...*

> ... *Consider living in this country, all our Asian minority. You don't know the people around you. If you have relatives, like mother, sister, when bad times come they will nevertheless help you.*

> *With an elder person around, children learn something more of the values of your culture, respect – i.e. how to greet each other on waking up etc.*

> *I lived with my parents until they died and I enjoyed life and they also enjoyed living with me ... If they go into an old people's home, no love there, nothing, just material comforts, no more than that. But if a sister or daughter or grandchildren are there then life is absolutely different and the children also enjoy elderly people.*

> *Looking at our family I think it is a good idea. The advantages are that we are all there for each other when we need anybody or anything, and the disadvantage is that sometimes you have your ups and downs between the ladies – between the aunties. Apart from that, it's pretty OK. You have fun and you have everybody round to talk to. You don't get bored and you're not lonely.*

Unmarried children should live at home

All single respondents were living with their parents.

Although respondents felt that it was OK for married children – particularly daughters – to live elsewhere, single children of whatever age were expected to reside with their parents. A single grown-up child living away from the parental home might go 'astray' and become a source of shame and anxiety.

> ... *it would feel unpleasant if your own child was living elsewhere. In the parents' mind there would be several kinds of worries, for*

parents, no matter how grown-up they are, to parents they are not grown-up, for parents it feels as if they are still little.

Changing living arrangements?

Some respondents suggested that the multi-generational model could only work if everyone liked each other and got on. Some families might live near to each other but be apart because of this.

The point is that if you could live in unity then it's an advantage, and if there are some families that bust up then its better that they live away from each other.

It depends upon their attitude. If they love each other, then that is a paradise. If they have no respect for each other or no patience to each other then it is better to live separately. If they can live close together then that is much better than living long distance.

Close but separate households

Older parents noted the attitude of their children and suggested they would only want to live with their children where that feeling was reciprocated.

I lived with my parents in the same house when I was married. Those were very good days. If I feel that my children's wives or their husbands – they feel not good [about us living there], I will not stay with them, even for a single day. It depends, if there is love, that's OK. If I feel there is a problem, it's not my right to stay with them.

We will live close by, one should give them freedom too, not enforce upon them, you have your self respect too. It is their lives too, one should give them freedom too – not hold them and say no, you must stay with us.

No, my wife would not like that either, ... say, my daughter's way of living with her husband may be completely different [to our way of living] I would not like to live there and put my foot in it.

A few (mainly younger) respondents felt it better to have parents living locally rather than within the household for reasons of privacy and autonomy. Overall, however, younger respondents were just as much in favour of living in an extended family as older respondents.

Living with siblings

Most respondents felt married siblings and their respective families should live near each other rather than within the same household, often citing rivalries and jealousy between siblings as reasons for this.

ATTITUDES TO MARRIAGE

All married respondents (20) had children. All but one respondent believed that marriage was very important, offering a stable environment for children and a deeper commitment between partners.

Cohabitation

None of our respondents had any experience of cohabitation, which they believed was unacceptable for Muslims in both cultural and religious terms. They felt it was a loose arrangement in which men were very likely to abandon women and children. They considered illegitimacy shameful, believing that it caused suffering for both children and parents.

Only one respondent felt it was permissible to have children outside marriage, but only if both parents were committed to each other and the relationship.

Arranged marriage

All married respondents had an 'arranged marriage', where their parents (and often other senior family members) chose the marriage partner. In most cases spouses had not been allowed to meet until the wedding, although at least four had married their cousins, whom they already knew. None had expected or had any input into pre-marital discussions, negotiations or preparations. Respondents neither expected, nor were given, a choice, but took it for granted that parents and family elders would make the best decision possible. Seven married respondents suggested that, given the choice, they would have preferred to postpone marriage until they were older. Men would have preferred to have a home or savings before entering marriage, while women felt they were too immature, and would have liked to have waited a few years.

Change

Nearly all respondents with unmarried children, regardless of age, expected them to have arranged marriages when the time came. However, most parents suggested they would allow their child to at least see their possible spouse and they would be given a degree of choice. A small number of parents were unsure whether their children would have an arranged marriage. This was partly related to their children being very young at the time of interview, and the concern that their children might become acculturated in the process of growing up in the UK.

Attitudes towards divorce

None of our respondents had been divorced, although one had been widowed and had remarried.

Most respondents felt that married couples should not divorce, under any circumstances. They believed that children suffered if parents divorced by seeing little of a father or mother. The children of divorced parents would also find it difficult to marry themselves, since no family would want to become involved with such a stigma. Overwhelmingly, respondents felt it better to stay together for the sake of the children.

One respondent suggested that, for Muslims, religious law dictates that it is the father, rather than the mother, who takes guardianship of the children. A mother getting divorced would therefore be forced to leave her children behind.

Those who did not disagree absolutely with divorce suggested it should only be considered in very rare and extreme cases. All felt that, regardless of the circumstances, the children of divorced parents would suffer.

WORK AND MONEY

Respondents had widely different economic circumstances. The men were either in full-time paid employment, part-time paid employment or were unemployed. Despite some attempt to obtain interviews from men in white-collar work, nearly all our respondents were in unskilled or semi-skilled manual work.

Women and work

- Only one woman was in work, and only one other woman had any experience of paid employment.

- All married women were housewives.

- The sole single woman respondent was prevented by her father from working or studying outside the home.

On women going to work

A few respondents (including some women) felt it was completely unacceptable for married women with children to go out to work. Another proportion of respondents were generally against it.

Most, however, felt that it was *permissible* (rather than wholly acceptable) for single women to work, particularly if they could work in female only environments. Fewer preferred a mixed-sex, all-Muslim environment. The least preferred option was a completely mixed environment.

A married woman's place is in the home

Nearly all respondents felt that, once married, a woman's job was in the home looking after her husband and children. Most respondents felt that children suffered emotionally and developmentally when mothers went to work We were told on more than one occasion that '*the mother is the child's first teacher*'.

Domestic responsibilities

None of the men we spoke to had any input into child care in the home or domestic labour. Those who were working outside of the home gave this as the main reason. Others suggested they did not have the necessary skills and therefore those tasks were best left to wives. Those without wives relied on mothers, sisters or older daughters to complete such tasks.

Men's responsibilities were much more connected to activities outside the home. Women were much less likely to enter public spaces than men – partly for reasons of culture, partly for fear of racial harassment and violence – and so men sometimes helped by doing the shopping and escorting children to school, the park and so on.

Men and money

Regardless of type of income, all monies, whether state benefits or wages, were usually held jointly and organised by the most senior man in the household – usually the husband, father or father-in-law.

CHILDREN

Gender roles

Almost all respondents felt that sons and daughters were treated equally in terms of affection and education. Perhaps because gender roles in the home were so rigidly divided and taken for granted by the adults, parents did not understand our question about gender roles and the differing expectations that parents might have from sons and daughters.

Education at school

Most parents had little contact with schools except on Parents' Evening or if specifically requested by teaching staff. Men were more likely to discuss the progress of their children and related matters with the teachers.

Most respondents attached special importance to religious instruction for their children within state schools. A small number of Bengalis wanted their children to learn Bengali at school, most of whom were already able to do so. One parent felt it important that his children had the opportunity to learn Arabic at school, and one Pakistani parent felt it unfair that Bengali was offered at school but not Urdu.

A number of respondents felt that Pakistani and Bangladeshi children should be offered a broadly based instruction about their history and culture within state schools. Discipline and respect for elders were also mentioned, but most parents were happy to do this informally.

Education at home

Nearly all respondents with children ensured they undertook some form of cultural activity. For most this focused on religious studies, which included reading the Qur'an – usually in Arabic – and perhaps also attendance at a mosque. Mothers often taught religion to the younger children at home, while respondents sometimes invited religious leaders into their homes to teach Arabic and religious instruction to the older ones.

CONTACT WITH FAMILY OUTSIDE THE HOUSEHOLD

Family in the UK

All respondents had some family living in the UK. Many had family living very near, in the same street or building, who were often seen or heard from every day. Most respondents wanted more contact with family living further away in the UK, but kept in touch by phone.

Family overseas

All but one respondent had family resident in Pakistan or Bangladesh and a smaller number had family in North America, the Middle East and other parts of Europe. Respondents kept in touch mainly by phone, although most respondents had visited or been visited by family from Pakistan or Bangladesh in the last five years.

A quarter of the households sent money to family in Bangladesh or Pakistan, generally to support aged parents, although presents to other relatives were also common, often as wedding gifts. Some households solely dependent upon state benefits regularly sent money to Bangladesh.

MIXED RELATIONSHIPS

Experience of mixed relationships

About half of the respondents had experience of mixed marriages or relationships within their own families or amongst friends. None felt the examples they had seen were positive.

Attitudes towards mixed relationships

The majority of our respondents were completely against the idea of Pakistanis and Bengalis marrying outside of their cultural and religious group, though most also suggested it would be acceptable if the 'outsider' were Muslim or was prepared to convert.

> *Whether Pakistani or Arabian or Jamaican or American, so long as the religion is Muslim [Islam]. If the religion is Muslim then you can go with anybody, there is no obstruction. But to relate to another religion, to mix with English [Christian], mix with the Jews. Amongst Jamaicans there are some English [Christian]. Other cultures have them. A Muslim can mix with a Muslim. There is no objection.*

Respondents' reasons for being against mixed marriages included:

* Religious incompatibility:

> *I will think it's bad. He is a person from another religion. This country is English, [Christian] is not my religion. He is not a Muslim. He is not doing Namaz, he is not fasting, he is not even reading Bismillah.* * *He is probably drinking his alcohol or behaving in another manner. How can I joyfully get on with him? To marry is you and I to join in matrimony in this world and life after. Now how can two religions be? That is anyhow bad.*

* Cultural difficulties:

> *From my point of view there'd be quite a few [disadvantages] because we are from a very strict background. Normally if you go into another religion or marry someone from a different culture all together you have a massive problem trying to adjust and if we had a White lady marrying into our family, she'd have a massive problem trying to adjust to my Dad's family – all the brothers, because they're really very strict. That's a disadvantage. But apart from that, the lady does all the sacrifices, adjusts, it's up to her once she's married into a different family – it's up to her to make it work.*

---

* 'Namaz' means prayer in Urdu; 'Bismillah', an Arabic word meaning 'In the name of Allah' , the invocation of God, is basic to Muslim prayers and is recited at the start of important activities.

> *Disaster... A Muslim and another ethnic cannot work, even if you do not consider it on religious basis, two cultures, two totally different cultures...*

- Instability:

> *I know of so many men that kept English women. They even kept them before marriage and then they left them and got married, or this woman left ... It was done but not by marrying. Without marrying, women were kept, had three, four children, do you understand? Some of their men died, some of the men left at the end. Some of them have women leaving for another man.*

- Damage to children:

> *The child would be confused. These children, you will not be able to bring them up in your ways, neither the partner's ways.*

> *I personally wouldn't at all feel very happy about it ... the cultural strength is cut off. Then he is just floating around and he doesn't know where he will end up. Their children, what we see these days as an ideal sort of example. It is not successful at all. The major point is that the children are torn apart, they do not know which culture or parts they should adopt.*

ATTITUDES TOWARDS OTHER ETHNIC GROUPS

Although a few respondents felt that they had something in common with the traditional family values of older Whites, most felt they had very little in common with White families. They had little contact with or direct knowledge of other ethnic groups in the UK. Respondents contrasted their own, close knit, families with White British families' emphasis on individual freedom:

> *Their thinking is different. We think in terms of holding our family together. We are always thinking of what is good for our families, they always think of themselves and their personal freedom. We always consider our family reputation/name before we act. Like that, they are more free thinking. The women are more liberal than our women.*

Some also highlighted differences in child-rearing practices:

> *I see two types of White families here. One, they give their children very good training, and one they are not caring about their children, they are destroying their children and those children are becoming a problem to the whole nation. If parents don't respect their children, then children don't respect their parents. They don't bother with each other, so those children, when they grow up, they will be a problem for the nation.*

It was not always that White parents did not care about their children, but that they did not have enough time to look after their children appropriately:

> *I don't think they have enough time to give to the families, but obviously you cannot generalise it. The older, good English families who still have a very traditional outlook and thinking, they are very similar to our outlook. But, definitely there is a problem, because both parents work, hardly give time to them [children], so what happens is that they float. Ours too [children], if we do not give time, ours too would float, i.e. do whatever they see on TV and outside.*

> *For example, if they are professional and earning well they think by having a nanny to look after their children while they are working and sending their children to private schools they feel they are doing all they can and they are providing the best thing, but I personally feel that there is something lacking. The time you should give to your children is more important.*

Most Bangladeshi families are similar to each other

Most Bengali respondents felt they shared most similarities with other Bengalis because of their religious beliefs, language, family organisation and personal conduct. Only two highlighted differences in the extent to which religious beliefs were practised. One said:

> *What can I say? I do Namaz and fast, some individuals are not keeping it... When I eat I check which is Halal. Some won't check, they'll eat anything. Some don't do their Namaz, go to the mosque. Him and me, there is a difference.*

Most Bengalis also felt they had much in common with other Muslims:

> *All Muslims are the same, we all believe in Allah, we all pray, women cover themselves, eat Halal food, no we are all OK, the same.*

Most Pakistani families are different from one another

Most Pakistani respondents felt there were differences between themselves and other Pakistani families. Only one respondent felt that they had much in common with other Asian families, which were different because of their culture and religion.

> *Every [Pakistani] family is different, some are more social, close, some are more traditional.*

> *You see there are many different types of Muslims. The Muslim in Saudi and Dubai are very different from Pakistani Muslims, even in Pakistan there are Urdu-speaking Muslims and Punjabi-speaking Muslims. I could not settle in Dubai.*

One respondent felt a growing gulf between herself and her Asian peers due to the strictness of her parents.

> *Me and my sister, we walk round with our heads covered and every-thing, and when we walk past a bunch of Indian girls they'll all be laughing, and when they see us their voices raise and if they're with guys they just jump around – they try to show off. I just don't understand it. We have quite a few White friends and they're pretty cool about us covering our heads and everything. I think the way we dress, and the way we cover our heads, we are accepted more by the Whites than by our own. I feel pretty awkward with my Asian friends if I see them on the street, I feel a bit uncomfortable, but if I bump into a White friend or I bump into my friends' families, that's OK. They accept us for covering our heads, but the Asian girls – I don't know, it's like 'you've got your head covered; you're like a little angel', but, you know it's like normal for me and my sister ...*

Changes in Pakistani families

One parent also suggested that things may be changing for the worst amongst some Pakistani young people.

[Pakistani children in the UK] they dress up so oddly, they compete with Whites. I say adopt the good things, nobody is stopping you, but the negative things, the unsuitable for you, you should not do it. Parents do not seem to have that control any more, they have left the children ... There are so many divorces in good families now. Today they get married, two weeks later ... Parents have not made the children very strong ... they have left them to the mercy of the situation.

Chapter 5

Ethnic Minority Families Compared

Having presented the views of our respondents on an ethnic grouping basis, in this chapter we pull together our findings so that the
views of different groups can be compared with each other. We also
include some responses from interviews with some White people so
that ethnic minority views can be seen alongside those of Whites.

MULTI-GENERATIONAL HOUSEHOLDS

South Asians

The preference for multi-generational households is differently felt
among the different South Asian groupings. Most – though not all –
Pakistanis and Bangladeshis felt that parents and their adult children
should live together, with married sons moving their wives in. They
felt this was an ideal solution for living, which fostered deep and
meaningful relationships, helped pass on cultural practices and
ensured that the family would function as a mutually rewarding
support system. Nearly a quarter of Pakistanis and Bangladeshis were
living in an extended family, with in-laws, siblings, or cousins, and
some others would like to have done so, if large enough accommo-
dation was available.

• Some older Pakistani and Bangladeshi parents felt that the
   attitude of children was changing, and that they would only want
   to live with their grown-up children if the feeling was reciprocated. A few preferred to live near, rather than with their grown
   up children. Indeed, one Pakistani parent felt that living with
   grown up children could be an inconvenience for both parties.

- Younger Pakistanis and Bangladeshis were generally as much in favour of living in an extended family as their older counterparts, though again a few felt it was better to have parents living locally rather than with the household for reasons of privacy and autonomy.

- Indian and African Asian parents, by contrast, believed that married children should set up home on their own but felt that they should remain nearby to look after their parents (though the Fourth National Survey of Ethnic Minorities found that the generations may come to live together in later years). In this, their views were much closer to the African-Caribbeans than to the other Asians.

- All unmarried children of South Asian parents, regardless of their age, were expected to live with their parents, who felt that they might become assimilated into a British culture, away from ethno-religious values and traditions. This would be a source of shame and anxiety.

African-Caribbeans

The overwhelming majority of African-Caribbean respondents did not want their parents living with them (despite the fact that the Fourth Survey found that a third of Caribbean elders lived with their adult children). They felt that breaking ties with home and parents was a positive way of building life and emotional skills. All individuals needed their own 'space' and privacy. 'Space' denoted a process of emotional distancing or separation, as well as a physical dimension. Few saw the possibility of benefits and additional support that elders might give to grown up children and grandchildren (in contrast to Hylton 1997).

Although they did not want to live with their parents, some African Caribbeans felt quite strongly that children owe their parents a debt that can be repaid in old age. Most preferred having parents living in the local area and most parents preferred to live locally. This was seen as the best of both worlds. Parents would be near enough to offer help and support when needed, but far enough away for their children to have privacy.

Marriage, cohabitation and divorce

South Asian groups displayed high levels of long-term and life-term marriage. By contrast, African-Caribbeans and Whites displayed not only a range of relationships but often movement between different types of relationship.

Both African-Caribbean and White groups included a number of single parents, some of whom were separated or divorced, and some of whom had never been married. None of the South Asians were single parents.

Attitudes to marriage and to bringing up children within marriage are important findings of the study for two reasons. Firstly, they seem to be the main issue on which there could be said to be a shared Asian view, for, as this chapter shows, on most matters the Pakistanis and Bangladeshis take a much more conservative or traditional view than the Indians and African Asians.

Secondly, the interviews suggest that even if statistically most African-Caribbean adults are not married, many more than actually do get married, aspire to marriage and do not regard other forms of relationships as meaningful as marriage.

Attitudes to marriage

- Almost all Asian respondents, even those who were single, regarded marriage as extremely important.

- Most African-Caribbean respondents had a positive attitude to marriage as an ideal to aspire to. They felt it was more important than living with someone.

South Asians: arranged marriages

Most South Asians had some form of arranged marriage. While no one who had had such an arrangement expressed any objections to arranged marriages, some wished they had been older before they were married. There were, however, clear differences between the two South Asian groupings. Yet in each grouping there was a shift towards more choice than had been the case before.

Pakistani and Bangladeshi respondents who were married had had no say in the process of selecting a spouse. They believed that their children too would have an arranged marriage when the time came. Most said, however, that they would allow their children to see a potential spouse, and that they would be prepared to give their children a degree of choice.

Most of the married Indians and African Asians, too, had had an arranged marriage. In their case, however, most had had some input into the selection process. Of the six unmarried Indians and East Africans, all but one believed that although they were likely to have an arranged marriage, they would have more say in the choice of partner.

Uncertainty

- A small number of Bangladeshi and Pakistani parents felt unsure whether their children would have an arranged marriage, partly because the children were still very young, and partly because they would grow up in the UK. About half the married Indians and East Africans were also uncertain about whether their children would have an arranged marriage.

- A minority of Indians and East Africans believed that their children were unlikely to have an arranged marriage.

Cohabitation

- South Asians perceived cohabitation as a loose arrangement in which men were very likely to abandon women and children. They considered illegitimacy shameful, and believed that both parents and children suffered as a result.

- Many African-Caribbeans who were currently single wanted to be married, but viewed cohabitation as a pragmatic 'first step' towards marriage. This view was generally echoed by Whites.

- A minority of African-Caribbeans felt there was little difference between marriage and cohabitation.

- Some African-Caribbeans and a few Whites believed that cohabitation was more likely to lead to relationship breakdown.

Children before marriage?

For most African-Caribbeans, the level of commitment between two individuals was more important than whether a relationship was socially or legally recognised. Making a commitment to children was not necessarily related to commitment between parents.

This view was not shared by South Asians.

African-Caribbeans and South Asians agreed, however, that marriage provided more stability for children and parents, as well as additional emotional benefits for children, including positive role models and an inner sense of confidence.

Marriage is fundamental

- Overwhelmingly, South Asians felt that marriage was important and normal, offering a stable environment for children and a deeper commitment between partners.

- Slightly less than half of African-Caribbeans felt that marriage conveyed additional security, and implied a stronger relationship than cohabitation.

Marriage is just a piece of paper

- All except three of the remaining African-Caribbeans felt that there was little difference between marriage and cohabitation. The level of commitment between individuals was the important factor.

- Three African-Caribbeans had no strong opinion, but felt that the decision to marry before having children depended on personal or religious preference.

Family pressure?

Neither African-Caribbeans nor Whites felt that their families minded their cohabiting. Most African-Caribbeans suggested that their families were more interested in their personal happiness than in their living arrangements. Whites suggested that families who were unhappy about cohabitation usually based their arguments on their religious beliefs.

Attitudes towards divorce

Divorce is always wrong

- Almost all Pakistanis and Bangladeshis felt that married couples should not divorce. They felt that divorce was socially, spiritually and morally unacceptable. Not only would children suffer through seeing little of one parent, they would also find it difficult to marry themselves, since other families would not want to be associated with the stigma of divorce. Overwhelmingly, respondents felt that it was better to stay together for the sake of the children, and that divorce was necessary only in very rare and extreme cases.

- About half the Indians and East Africans also felt that divorce was unacceptable, because of the adverse effects on children.

- A few African-Caribbeans felt that divorce was only permissible under extreme circumstances, such as physical cruelty. Only two believed that divorce was not permissible under any circumstances.

Divorce is sometimes acceptable

- About half the Indians and East Africans supported individuals' right to divorce. Like those against divorce, these respondents supported their arguments by referring to the detrimental effects on children. Staying together would make a bad situation worse, especially if there were children involved. Some respondents believed it was more difficult for Indians to divorce due to cultural constraints, such as the pressure brought to bear by the community.

- Most African-Caribbeans and Whites felt that divorce was permissible under a whole range of circumstances, where the couple were unhappy together and unable to get on. Most felt that it was better to divorce than stay in an unhappy relationship, when the effect on the children would be worse, though a minority believed that parents should stay together until the children grew up.

Gender differences in expectations

African-Caribbeans and Whites believed that there were gender differences in expectations about marriage. African-Caribbeans generally felt that marriage was more important for women in terms of security and as an accomplishment signifying maturity. By contrast, Whites felt that marriage offered greater security for men rather than women.

For African-Caribbeans, who were two-thirds women:

- men benefited from marriage in a functional way, getting regular meals, washing done and regular sex;

- men accrued additional responsibility from marriage rather than additional benefits;

- women gained increased commitment from partners and increased social status among friends and family.

The White sample was also two thirds women. Only half of all White respondents felt that marriage was a positive achievement for women. The remainder believed that:

- marriage was more advantageous for men, in both functional terms and in terms of emotional security;

- by getting married, women lost their autonomy, independence and freedom to make both small and large choices in their lives.

Gender, generation or religion?

- Nearly all Whites felt that their attitude to marriage was different from that of their parents, and most felt that their own children would have different views from their own.

- A minority of Whites suggested that generation differences were more important than gender in expectations of marriage; negative attitudes towards cohabitation and illegitimacy were associated with a particular generation.

- A minority of African-Caribbeans felt that it was not gender but religion which was the decisive factor, with marriage being more important to the religious than to the non-religious.

GENDER ROLES IN AND OUTSIDE THE HOME

The domestic division of labour

In the majority of households visited, domestic labour was unevenly divided, with women taking the larger share of household tasks. There was little suggestion that men were actively sharing domestic labour, regardless of whether either or both parties were working outside the home. It was only among the few White households that were interviewed that the wives and mothers appeared to be doing less domestic labour than their ethnic minority counterparts. This was partly because White men were more willing to share housework, and in White homes paid help was more likely to be used.

Pakistanis and Bangladeshis

Only one of the women was currently in paid employment outside the home, and only two women had experience of working outside the home.

None of the men did any childcare at home or domestic labour. They said this was because they went out to work and/or they did not have the necessary skills. The men helped with childcare outside the home, such as escorting children to school and discussing school matters with teachers.

Indians and East Africans

Among Indians and East Africans there were almost twice as many women as men. About half of all respondents were in paid employment; a third were in full-time education, with the remainder looking after children or retired.

- Women did the cooking and cleaning, and ensured the smooth running of the household, even where they were in paid employment.

- Men justified their minimal role by suggesting that their partners had taken the lead in determining this division of labour.

- Women appeared to accept this situation.

African-Caribbeans

Eighteen of a total of 24 African-Caribbeans in 19 households were women; all but six of the respondents were in paid employment.

- Domestic labour was usually carried out by women, regardless of commitments outside the home.

- Only one man, a single parent, claimed to do his own domestic labour. Another suggested that the domestic labour was shared between the couple, while another said he did the cooking and his wife did the rest.

Whites

Arrangements in White households contrasted strongly with the rest of the respondents.

- Around a quarter of these households employed domestic cleaners, who did the bulk of the household labour.

- In about a fifth of households, respondents suggested that domestic labour was shared, with men doing the cooking rather than the cleaning.

- In another fifth, respondents suggested that a traditional divide was maintained, with men doing little if any domestic labour.

Women and work

Most respondents in all groups, except Pakistanis and Bangladeshis, thought it was permissible for women to be in paid employment outside the home. There were mixed feelings about this, however, as many also felt that the age of a woman's children and the financial circumstances of the family were important factors. The younger the children and the wealthier the family, the less likely were respondents to favour work outside of the home for the mother.

Pakistanis and Bangladeshis

- Nearly half of Pakistanis and Bangladeshis (who were three-quarters men) felt that a married woman's job was in the home looking after the family.

- Some others felt it was completely unacceptable for married women with children to go out to work.

- Most also felt, however, that it was permissible, rather than wholly acceptable, for single women to work, particularly if they could work in wholly female environments.

Indians, East Africans, African-Caribbeans and Whites

In contrast with Pakistanis and Bangladeshis, many in these groups (among whom there were more women than men) felt that women *should* go out to work. Most women believed that a second wage earner was crucial to the maintenance of a decent standard of living for the family. Indeed, White women seemed to take work for granted, and saw the decision about whether to combine work with children as a mother's personal choice.

- African-Caribbean women felt that work gave women a degree of financial independence. White women felt it boosted women's morale and self-esteem.

- Some thought that women should only work once the children were at school, though most saw combining work with children as a matter of personal decision.

CHILDREN

Formal education

Overall, Whites, Indians and East Africans were the most satisfied with their children's education and African-Caribbeans least satisfied.

- Most African-Caribbeans felt that their children should be taught Black history or culture, or have lessons that would help build a positive identity, confidence or self respect.

- A smaller number of African-Caribbeans felt that their children should learn about other cultures, nationalities or religions, as well as their own.

- Pakistani and Bangladeshi parents were most concerned about their children having access to Islamic teaching.

Cultural activities (other than religion)

- Most Indian, East African and Caribbean parents suggested that their children did not take part in any distinctive cultural activities. Many Caribbean parents nevertheless wished to have Black history taught in schools.

RELIGIOUS DIVERSITY

Muslims

Nearly all Pakistani and Bangladeshi parents ensured that their children undertook some form of cultural or religious activity.

- For most this meant reading the Qu'ran (usually in Arabic). Religious study was often undertaken at home, with younger children instructed by their mother, while older children might be taught by religious leaders invited into the home to teach both Arabic and religion.

Hindus and Sikhs

- Religion was most important to Hindus, providing a moral code for living, involving daily prayer and influencing what they ate and drank.

- Only a small number of Hindus felt that religion was not important in their daily lives.

- Some Sikhs interpreted the influence of religion in negative terms, feeling that it constrained the choices available to individuals.

Christians

A third of African-Caribbean children took part in activities related to the church or religion. Activities included Sunday school, participation in religious playgroups, church after-school clubs or religious studies at home under parental instruction.

ETHNIC AND CULTURAL DIVERSITY

Most respondents from ethnic minorities felt they had little in common with White families. They felt that they had close extended families which operated as a unit, in contrast to White families which concentrated on the individual and personal freedom at the expense of the family. Pakistanis and Bangladeshis emphasised respect for elders and parents, and saw White parents as having little control over their children. A few felt that the traditional families of older Whites had something in common with their own values. The ethnic minority groups also thought they were very different from each other.

- Most Bangladeshis felt they were most similar to other Bangladeshis, as well as to other Muslims. Although a minority felt that they differed from both other Bengali families and other Muslims, none of this group felt that they had anything in common with any other ethnic group in Britain, although most did not know anyone who was not a Bengali or a Muslim.

- Most Pakistanis, by contrast, stressed the differences between themselves and other Pakistani families.

- Indians and African Asians particularly stressed their differences from African-Caribbean families. They saw African-Caribbeans as similar to Whites, having totally different values and attitudes to religion, family and education.

Difference from White British people

Most ethnic minority respondents felt that they had very little in common with White families, citing numerous examples of differences:

- South Asians and a few Caribbeans felt that White families concentrated on the individual at the expense of the family unit, whereas their own families were closely knit.

- A majority in all minority groups felt that White parents had no control over their children, whereas their own families valued discipline and respect for elders and parents above all.

- South Asians highlighted differences related to religious beliefs, such as rules relating to food and drink. They felt that religion was more important to them than to Whites.

- Two African-Caribbeans believed that religion was a more important difference between themselves and White people than culture.

Attitudes towards mixed relationships

While most Pakistanis and Bangladeshis were against the idea of marrying outside their cultural and religious group, there was little opposition among Indians and East Africans. There appeared to be slightly less antipathy among ethnic minorities to mixed relationships with White people than with other ethnic groups.

Pakistanis and Bangladeshis

- Most felt marrying out was acceptable only if the prospective partner were Muslim or prepared to become a Muslim.

- A small number felt that culture and family background were as important as whether the prospective partner was Muslim, and that mixed marriages would have to overcome many difficulties.

Indians and African Asians

- There was little objection to mixed relationships among this group, though this was qualified by the recognition that such relationships had particular difficulties. These included cultural difficulties and the fact that the children would be subject to racism from both sides.

- Single respondents had open views about mixed relationships, reporting direct experience of relationships outside their own ethnic group.

African-Caribbeans

- Most African-Caribbeans did not object to mixed relationships and some were positive about them.

- A very large minority, however, had negative views about mixed relationships in general. Most of those who disapproved were against relationships with White people, while a smaller number felt uncomfortable about any type of mixed relationships (these proportions being much larger than in the Fourth Survey).

- Those who were against mixed relationships thought that they were bad for children, possibly leading to confusion about identity.

- They strongly disapproved of those who used mixed relationships to 'get on'.

- Some felt that culture and colour were less important than love and respect.

- Others welcomed mixed relationships, feeling that they broke down barriers in society and gave the children of such relationships a richer heritage than they otherwise would have.

Whites

Amongst the White interviewees, more than half of either had no objection to mixed relationships or held positive views about them.

Chapter 6

Accommodating both Individualism and Familyism

The three groupings studied here all exhibit change and reflect internal variety of attitudes and circumstances. While most respondents did not seem unduly dissatisfied with their lifestyles, nor did their comments suggest that they perceive themselves to be participating in a 'relationship revolution'. In some cases people felt that the kind of partnerships and co-parenting that they sought were not being achieved. Yet the contrasts between the three groupings, as highlighted in the previous chapter, suggest that the differences in attitudes and norms are as striking as the differences captured in the statistics summarised in the Appendix.

The Pakistanis and Bangladeshis in this study were all in unskilled or semi-skilled work, or unemployed or, especially the women, were economically inactive. Nearly all were married, of whom all had had an arranged marriage in which they had had no say, and marriage was seen as unambiguously a life-term commitment. They aspired to live in multi-generational households, in which upon marriage the groom would bring his wife to join his parents' household, and regretted that the households could not be larger. There may be an element of nostalgia or myth-making as most did not currently live in such households. Nevertheless, all household income was held jointly and managed by the senior male of the household, and remittances were sent to elderly parents who were not living with their children. A traditional division of labour by gender prevailed. The majority view was that married women should be at home, and working women should work in female environments (see also Metcalf, Modood and Virdee 1996). The men gave limited help with childcare or housework. The critical cultural activities were associated with Islam, and there was concern that religious instruction was not available at school. They thought of themselves as very different from White families and disapproved of Muslims 'marrying out'. The British cultural environment – as observed on television, rather than by close personal engagement – is seen as a threat to the cohesion and norms of Pakistani and Bangladeshi families. When White Britons talk of 'the breakdown of the family' they are thinking of the nuclear family; when these Asians worry about what is happening to 'the family' they point to the challenges to the network of authority and loyalty consisting of multi-generational households, the extended family, the authority of elders and arranged marriage.

While these respondents were unashamedly traditional, there were movements in their attitudes. A minority expressed a preference for younger families living in separate households to their parents, though in the same neighbourhoods, and there was some division of opinion about whether women should have paid work outside the home. Probably the biggest movement was the expectation that marrying couples should have some say in arranged marriages.

In this the African Asians and Indians were perhaps a generation ahead of them, for while they believed in the importance of marriage, preferably for life, negotiated arranged marriages had become the norm. But even this was considered too restrictive among some of the younger people (see also Francome 1994). While they emphasised the importance of obeying and respecting one's elders, the expectation was that adult children should live with parents until they were married but not necessarily thereafter, though the two households might join again when the parents were elderly and not able to look after themselves. These Asians were happy with women in paid employment outside the home, but expected traditional gender roles to be observed inside the home. They thought that White people were quite different from themselves but did not express much opposition to intermarriage with Whites; it was some of the other minorities that were considered less acceptable (see also IPPR 1997).

Our Caribbean interviewees expressed much greater hostility to mixed relationships with White partners than found by the Fourth Survey. They expressed an anxiety that having a White partner was seen as being essential to upward mobility and sent out a message that one's own community was not good enough for one (Modood,

Beishon and Virdee 1994). They also said that their own communities were more family-orientated than the White British and instilled more discipline and respect for age than their White contemporaries. Indeed, there was unity among the minorities in their criticism of what they perceived as a lack of commitment to parenting amongst Whites and they talked of White children as not having respect for their parents and elders, and as being out of control. These findings echo those of another recent project on ethnic minority families. The Moyenda project, also supported by the Joseph Rowntree Foundation, took the view that despite the differences between various groups (which, in their case, included Africans), there are important commonalities between what are referred to as 'Black' or 'visual minority' groups (Hylton, 1997). Focusing on parenting and, in particular, on how parents cope with the pressures of being ethnic minority parents and passing on the values and identities of their group, they found a common resistance to the pressures of 'UK liberalism', that is to say, an excessive individualism and materialism, in which personal gratification and fulfilment undermine more family-orientated values. The positive side of this commonality was that, first, the minorities had a religious or spiritual approach to life; second, they had a positive sense of extended family or kinship in which people welcome multi-generational households and relationships, and in which, for example, age is valued as a source of wisdom. The study's message was that 'survival is easier where people manage to hold onto a fairly consistent philosophy and view of the world' such as an Afrocentric way of life, or Islam (Hylton 1997: 4).

While there were features in our findings about Caribbeans consistent with the Moyenda study, other features were in stark contrast. This arose from the fact that the Caribbean respondents reflected a greater variety of attitudes and relationships than the other groupings. Some Caribbeans in fact emphasised an individualism – the importance of individual choice, the value of commitments generated by the quality of relationships rather than custom, duty or a marriage certificate, and independence – which resonated with the views of the White interviewees. It was noticeable, though, that the ideal of marriage and joint parenting between resident fathers and mothers still exerted a considerable appeal among the Caribbeans. Yet, for half the Caribbean respondents, whatever the ideal, fathers were in practice dispensable. There was no particular role or responsibility that fathers performed which could not be carried out in their absence by mothers. Mothers could and would fill any vacuum created by the (partial) absence of the father. Some of the respondents did not even know the whereabouts of their fathers. For a minority of Caribbeans, marriage has come to be regarded as just a lifestyle option, which one may or may not wish to choose, depending on individual circumstances. For the majority, however, marriage is an ideal which unfortunately only some achieve – mainly because, in the view of the women, men lack commitment. Given that Caribbean women are getting married later, and significant numbers are not marrying at all, the balance between these two outlooks on marriage and parenting may be shifting; but it does seem at the moment that the extent of Caribbean single mothering is driven more by difficulties in achieving an ideal that is still valued, rather than by alternative ideals. In this respect, our findings seem to concur with those of another recent Joseph Rowntree Foundation-supported study (Dench 1996).

Our Caribbean respondents were disproportionately female, and our sample sizes do not allow for rigorous generalisations, but it is clear that our interviews found a real concern about a lack of male commitment to long-term partnerships, and of 'marrying out' as betokening a lack of commitment to the Black community.

For South Asians, in contrast, fathers were head of the family, and the family came before individuals – or at least the interests of the family and the interests of individual members had to be reconciled, and the latter could not automatically take precedence over the former. It is highly unlikely that marriage and residential fathers will, for Asians, become 'just an option' in the foreseeable future. The ideology of life-term marriages and traditional gender complementarity was virtually without critics amongst the Asian respondents. There are changes taking place amongst Asians but they are changes to the conception of marriage, not the creation of alternatives to marriage. The direction of changes is such that British Asian families may be moving towards the two-parent nuclear family (with perhaps a grandparent) that was typical of Britain in the 1950s, rather than catching up with the relationship revolution of the post-1950s.

Gender asymmetry

There is a real sense in which the individualism of the Caribbeans and the familyism of the Asians place extra costs on women. In the former, women have to get on with the business of parenting and earning a living, whether their children's father is around or has exercised his individual freedom by remaining semi-detached or moving on to other relationships. In the case of some Asian families, women are confined to the domestic sphere; in others, they are expected to pursue qualifications and careers, but in both cases they typically get little help from their husbands in childcare or house-keeping. Hence, in their different ways, each of these arrangements puts the burden of parenting on mothers and in so far as it is shared, it is usually with other female relatives – mothers and sisters. That is not to say that these models of parenting are as good as each other – they certainly were not so in the opinion of the respondents. Rather, it is that each kind of relationship – traditional or revolutionary – is based on its own version of gender assymetery. There is no expecta-tion in any group that male and female behavioural differences are about to alter significantly.

An emergent multiculturalism

As these minorities are now part of the British social environment, some interaction between different orientations is inevitable. It has been argued that the Caribbeans have pioneered lifestyles (more economically independent women, more able and willing to take responsibility for children, less attached to the fathers of their children) that have influenced the younger generation of Whites; it has also been argued that the direction of influence has been the other way round and has had a destructive effect on Caribbean families (Dench 1996; Hylton 1997; James-Fergus 1997). Interviewing Asians certainly does not suggest that they believe they have influenced British relationships. Even though 'Asian family values' are ocassionally held up as a model for the rest of Britain (*Daily Mail* editorial, 9 August 1996), it is much easier to see how Asians are being more influenced than they are influencing; how they are trying to preserve while adapting. On the other hand, there is evidence that as the 'new British' begin to become civic players they will, like everyone else, seek to influence public norms and the political agenda. In this respect it is notable that the May 1997 General Election saw for the first time a guidance document produced by a broad-based national Muslim organisation highlighting issues of concern to Muslims (UKACIA, 1997). A priority of this document was greater support for the traditional family.

An irony worth noting here is that while the Qur'an allows a man, under certain conditions, to have up to four wives at a time, in practice urban Muslims throughout the world have become strictly monogamous and hostile to the culture of 'permissiveness' that is tolerant of multiple partnering. Western societies like Britain, on the other hand, have become tolerant of a man living with, and fathering children with, any number of women as long as he does not marry more than one of them at a time. This perhaps gives an inkling of the kind of debates and challenges that multicultural society will give rise to (Parekh 1995).

Multiculturalism is sometimes taken to be an aspect of the changes stemming from the 'relationship revolution', part of a new diversity which represents a movement away from the traditional ways of partnering and parenting, especially of the 'nuclear family' model of the 1950s. We suggest, however, that as a broad principle it seems that multiculturalism has to be about both supporting and allowing unfamiliar and innovative individualistic lifestyles, including alternatives to monogamy, and to supporting what may be called 'conservative' family forms. Appropriate concerns for public policy might be whether the various forms of living are a product of real choices, especially on the part of women, and whether they provide a basis for appropriate security and care for children and their development into responsible adults. Where there may be anxiety on either of these scores – whether the adult relationships were genuinely consensual and whether they were a good basis for bringing up children – then it may be appropriate for public policy interventions. Even then, it has to be borne in mind that the 'costs' of intervention would have to be weighed against the 'costs' of non-intervention. 'Costs' here does not primarily refer to finance, but to implications for conflicts within communities, 'race relations', state authoritarianism and so on.

Discussions about multiculturalism either picture it as a society of culturally-mixed individuals or as a group of distinct communities (Modood, 1998). The larger research from which this study has issued suggests that minority ethnicity today is taking the form of 'second generation' persons who do not necessarily participate in the cultural practices of their parents' generation but are shaping new mixed cultural practices and identities. But it is also taking the form of ethno-religious communities which have put down roots in Britain and are reproducing themselves. Some people may be more favourably inclined to one rather than the other of these developments. It would be mistaken and divisive, however, to identify one of these developments as positive and the other as negative. Both have a legitimate claim to make upon society. Policy which ignores the new salience of religious identification – for example, in relation to education, social services and the welfare of children – may fail to meet the needs of groups such as Muslims, Hindus and Sikhs. On the other hand, when some second and third generation persons are becoming relatively independent of their communities and the support that communities and families can offer, service provision cannot be premised on the idea that ethnic minority individuals have more informal support to draw on than their white peers. This means that policies in a multicultural society have to be genuinely sensitive to the 'multi' and not assume a homogeneity amongst the non-white population. This makes multicultural policy-making very complicated but we know of no way in which this can be avoided. We believe, therefore, that the sooner there is a general recognition of what diversity means, the sooner we can move away from positions that over-generalise.

The benefits of acknowledging the diverse character of ethnic minority families extend to theory too. It has been argued the relationship revolution since the 1960s, while connected to broader social and economic changes, is crucially a product of adults in western societies seeking new and more meaningful forms of intimacy and is, therefore, to be welcomed (Giddens 1992). Smart (1997) points out that the idea that a relationship is only worth being in while it promises a level of intimacy that cannot be bettered elsewhere is a perspective on families as if children did not exist. It is a perspective which also ignores the fact of migration and its consequences. Within it, the formations studied here are seen as being *in* Britain but not *of* Britain. We need, however, a view of contemporary Britain in which ethnic minority families are seen as integral and not just as 'deviant' or 'exotic'. Indeed, by taking ethnic minorities seriously, one might find a corrective to over-generalising theories about families. For it is unlikely to be the case that it is only among ethnic minorities that there will be people who are not so much seeking one-to-one forms of intimacy, but for whom family means a network of support, care, responsibility and loyalty that can allow each member to flourish and an identifiable way of life, usually connected with a cultural heritage, ethical ideals and an organised religion, to be maintained and renewed.

Appendix

Diverse Families in Britain

The Fourth National Survey of Ethnic Minorities is a key source for identifying the diverse family formations in Britain, and the one we rely on. Fieldwork was undertaken by ethnically matched interviewers in 1994. Over 5000 persons were interviewed from six minority groups: Caribbeans, Indians, African Asians (people of South Asian descent whose families had spent a generation or more in East Africa), Pakistanis, Bangladeshis and Chinese. Additionally, nearly 3000 White people were interviewed, so that comparison could be made of the circumstances of the minorities with those of the ethnic majority. Further details on all aspects of the survey are available in Modood et al., 1997, which should be seen, especially Chapters 2 and 9, as an essential companion to the present book. Some key findings from the Fourth Survey are presented below.

Ethnic minority families have to be seen in the context of the norms and experiences of migrant groups and their settlement in Britain, but also, of course, social trends in the UK.

Partnerships

Marital partnerships have been changing rapidly in Britain (Ermisch, 1983; Joshi, 1989; Buck et al., 1994). The pattern in the 1950s was that men and women married early and remained together for life. While that model still describes a large number of couples in the 1990s, both men and women have been marrying later than before. A high proportion of marriages end in separation or divorce, though many of the men and women involved marry again. Cohabitation has increased rapidly, especially among the most recent cohorts of young people. Research suggests that such relationships are of much shorter duration than marriage, indeed, many cohabitations are a prelude to marriage, though some take the form of a long-term alternative to marriage (Kiernan and Eastaugh, 1993; McRae, 1993). Some of these changes have gone much further in Britain than in many other industrialised countries, though broadly similar changes have taken place in most western countries (Dormor, 1992).

Drawing on the Fourth Survey, we can see, however, there are some striking differences between groups in Britain. People of Caribbean origin were much more likely to have remained single than Whites or South Asians. Nearly three-quarters of South Asians were in a formal marriage, compared with three-fifths of Whites, but only two-fifths of Caribbeans. Formal marriage was still the most common single outcome for Caribbeans, but only 39 per cent of 16- to 59-year-olds had adopted it. Younger Caribbeans were particularly unlikely to be married. Young Pakistanis and Bangladeshis (aged 20 to 24) were seven times as likely to be formally married as young Caribbeans.

Cohabitation and separation/divorce were both more common among Caribbean and White people than among those of Asian origin.

Cohabitation

Eighteen per cent of Caribbean couples and 11 per cent of White couples described themselves as 'living as married'. The proportion was much lower for all the Asian groups – between two and four per cent. It is interesting that the rate of cohabitation was similar for Caribbeans and Whites in their early 20s and those over the age of 40; the 'extra' Caribbean informal partnerships were mainly between the ages of 25 and 39.

Separation, divorce and widowhood

Of those who had ever been married, 18 per cent of Caribbean people had split up from their former partners (without remarrying). The proportion was down to nine per cent of White people but only four per cent of Asians.

The most striking difference, then, between the Caribbeans and others was the tendency of Caribbeans to live in single-adult households. Less than 40 per cent of 25–29-year-old Caribbeans had a live-in partner (compared to nearly 70 per cent of Whites), and less than 60 per cent of 30–34-year-olds had one, compared to 85 per cent of Whites and 94 per cent of Asians.

Mixed-ethnicity partnerships

A fifth of Caribbean adults who said they were either married or living as married had a White partner, compared to only four per cent of Indians and African Asians, and just one per cent of Pakistanis and Bangladeshis. Men were twice as likely as women to have a White partner.

The proportions in mixed relationships were much higher amongst those born in Britain: half of British-born Caribbean men, and a third of women, had chosen a White partner. Among the Indians and African Asians (who, as a group, came to Britain half a generation later than the Caribbeans), 19 per cent of British-born men, and ten per cent of women, had a White partner, though hardly any British-born Pakistanis or Bangladeshis had White partners.

Marriage is an important indicator of the distinctness of different ethnic identities. There was virtually no sign that the various minorities saw each other as forming a common pool from which to select non-White partners. There was some intermarriage between Indians and African Asians, but most of the latter said that their families had originally come from India. There were very few partnerships involving both Caribbeans and Asians, or between other Asian groups. There was not a single couple of mixed Pakistani-Bangladeshi origin.

Attitudes

The Fourth Survey included questions on people's attitudes to 'marrying out'. Asked whether their group would mind a close relative marrying a White person, a small majority of Caribbeans thought people from their group would not mind, but most South Asians thought it would be minded. It was among the Pakistanis that most thought that it would be minded (72 per cent) and the least among the Bangladeshis (50 per cent), but they also found it difficult to answer the question (25 per cent).

About a quarter to a third in each group said that, even though most of their group minded, they personally did not. This meant that, except in the case of the Pakistanis, a majority in each group said they personally did not mind, with more than four out of five Caribbeans expressing this view.

Attitudes of Whites

Amongst White people, a third thought that White people would not mind if a close relative were to marry an ethnic minority person, while just over half thought it would be minded, with more than a quarter saying it would be minded very much. Only a quarter of White people, however, said that they themselves would mind, which is half of what the British Social Attitudes surveys were finding in the 1980s (Young 1992,185); amongst 16–34-year-olds just over ten per cent said they would mind, suggesting that the future rate of inter-marriage may well come to be determined by the diverse attitudes held by the different minorities.

Partnerships between men and women from different ethnic groups will eventually have implications for the definition and concept of ethnic identity. In this regard, while White-Asian mixed children formed about two per cent of all children in Asian house-holds, four out of ten Caribbean children living with their parents had one White parent.

Arranged marriages: South Asians

A majority of South Asians over the age of 35, excluding African Asians, had their spouses chosen by their parents. This practice is most common among Pakistanis and Bangladeshis, with whom it is still the majority, albeit declining, arrangement among the young. The majority of Sikhs (56 per cent) too were married in this way, but not Hindus (36 per cent). The practice has been even less common among the African Asians and is now the exception among younger members of that group. It is now also a minority practice among younger Indians (27 per cent) and Sikhs (32 per cent), marking a very significant generational shift.

The survey findings show not only that the attitudinal changes are continuing to move in the same direction, but are also now beginning strongly to show themselves in how young married people describe the role of their parents in the choice of their spouse. Many respondents do not see the issues in the stark terms of 'parents' decision' and 'my decision', and it is clear that, even where individuals make their own decision, parents are closely involved (perhaps in even introducing the prospective partner). Nevertheless, the traditional parentally arranged marriage is in decline, consultation and negotiation are prevalent, and most young Hindus and Sikhs are now, at least in their own estimation, the final arbiters in the choice of their marriage partner.

Parents and children

Overall trends in child-rearing patterns since the 1950s have been as marked as those affecting marriage and cohabitation (Ermisch, 1990; Joshi, 1989; Buck et al., 1994). In the population as a whole, there have been two types of change: one relating to the number of children per family, the other to the number of parents.

Women have tended to have their first child later, and to have fewer children in total, than used to be the case. Although there has been some rise in the proportion of women who have no children at all, the most striking effect of the trend has been a reduction in the number of large families. This is well illustrated by statistics about family allowance and child benefit – the state payments for all families with children. In 1965, 232,000 families with five or more dependent children claimed benefit, but in 1995 this number had fallen to 77,000. The number with six or more children fell from 94,000 to 17,000 (DHSS, 1966; DSS, 1996a). Thus the 'large family', which had been the object of concern on such issues as overcrowding (e.g. Land, 1969), has practically disappeared from public discussion.

The second main national trend has been the growth of the number of one-parent families. This was already an issue in the early 1970s, when an official committee reported on the policy implications (Finer, 1974), but the total number has risen from 500,000 in 1971 to 1.3 million in 1993 (Haskey, 1993). During the earlier part of the period, the increase consisted principally of divorced and separated families; more recently, the number of families with a never-married mother has risen more rapidly, though they still account for less than half the total.

The Fourth Survey found that within these overall figures there were important differences by ethnicity. For example, ethnic minority couples were more likely to have children. Only about half of White couples where the wife was aged between 20 and 59 had dependent children. The proportion was nearer three-fifths for Caribbean and two-thirds for Indian and African Asian couples. Nearly four-fifths of Pakistani and nearly nine out of ten Bangladeshi couples had children.

Size of family

Pakistani and Bangladeshi families stood out as being far larger than others. Thirty-three and 42 per cent of them respectively had four or more children. Many of them (seven and nine per cent respectively) had six or more. Most of these children were born in Britain.

While cohabiting White couples were rather less likely to have children than fully married White couples, this was not true for Caribbeans – if anything, the cohabiters were more likely to have children than the married couples. These findings are consistent with the suggestion that White couples tend to treat cohabitation as a stage which will be converted into full marriage when, or after, children have been born; but that Caribbean couples tend not to move on to marriage in this way.

While very few Asian women had children and never married, this applied to one in six of White women between the ages of 20–59 with children. For Caribbean women, however, there was no special relationship between having children and marriage: they were nearly as likely to have children whether they were ever to marry (53 per cent) or not (47 per cent).

Caribbean women were also more likely to start having children at an earlier age. A higher proportion of them had children in their teens or early twenties than either White or Indian/African Asian women. At the teenage stage, more Caribbean women had had babies than even Pakistani and Bangladeshi women. Over the later age ranges, the proportion of Caribbeans with children was very similar to

Whites and Indian/African Asians. But in every age group up to the forties, Caribbean mothers were less likely than others to be married or cohabiting.

While 40 per cent of single Caribbean women had a child under 16 living with them, ten per cent of single Caribbean men said, in answer to a direct question, that they had a child under 16 who did not live with them. (Only 1.5 per cent of single White men said this.) This provides an indication that a majority of the children were either unknown to or denied by their fathers (unless each of the men had had children by several women). Nevertheless, it also suggests that a proportion of the children may have had at least some form of paternal relationship.

When lone mothering is combined with 'marrying out' it means that only a small number of children of Caribbean stock are being directly raised by two Black parents – less than a third of the total – suggesting that many children will grow up without the opportunity to observe closely the cultural and other characteristics of Caribbean men and women.

Multi-generational households

As many as one fifth of South Asian couples lived with (one of) their families; nearly a third of couples where the man was aged 30 would be living in their parental home. This was in spite of the fact that most of the people concerned had been born in Asia or Africa, and not all of them would have had the chance to live with their parents in Britain. In fact, analysis showed that if parents were resident in Britain, even amongst adults aged over 30, a quarter of South Asians lived with their parents compared to six per cent of Whites. A further distinctive feature is that the great majority of the South Asian couples living with the older generation were found in the same household as the man's parents. Among the few White or Black couples who lived with one set of parents, the woman's parents were chosen more often than the man's.

Only 13 per cent of Whites in their sixties or seventies shared a household with a son or daughter. A third of Caribbean elders lived with an adult child, and two-thirds of Asian elders were in this situation.

Changes over time

When the Fourth Survey data were compared with its predecessor, which was undertaken in 1982, it was evident there have been some clear changes over the last decade:

- a reduction in the average number of adults in Caribbean households. This almost certainly signifies a trend towards more Caribbeans living on their own (or with just their children);

- a slight fall in the number of adults in Indian and African Asian households, but a substantial rise in Pakistani and Bangladeshi households;

- a reduction in the average number of children in Indian households;

- fewer children, too, in Pakistani households, although the average has held steady in Bangladeshi households.

Economic circumstances

Certain economic circumstances should be noted, as they interact with household characteristics:

- Over 80 per cent of Bangladeshi women were looking after the home or family, as were 70 per cent of Pakistani women. Around a quarter of White and African Asian women were in this position, a third of Indians but only 13 per cent of Caribbeans.

- White women in work were much more likely to be in part-time work than ethnic minority women.

- Bangladeshis, Pakistanis and Caribbeans have very high levels of male unemployment, as well as higher than average levels of female unemployment.

- Caribbean, Indian and African Asian households were all more likely to be in poverty, and less likely to have relatively high family incomes, than Whites. The poverty amongst Pakistanis and Bangladeshis, however, was of a different magnitude: four out of five of these households were in poverty.

References

Buck, N, Gershuny, D, Rose, D and Scott, J (1994) *Changing Households: the British Household Panel Survey*, Colchester: University of Essex

Coote, A, Harman, H and Hewitt, P (1998) 'Family Policy: Guidelines and Goals' in Franklin, F (ed) *Social Policy and Social Justice: The IPPR Reader*, Cambridge: Polity Press

Dench, G (1996) *The Place of Men in Changing Family Cultures*, London: Institute of Community Studies

Dench, G (ed) (1997) *Rewriting the Sexual Contract*, London: Institute of Community Studies

Department of Health and Social Security (1996) *Social Security Statistics 1996*, London: HMSO

Dormor, D (1992) *The Relationship Revolution: Cohabitation, Marriage and Divorce in Contemporary Europe*, London: One Plus One

Ermish, J (1983) *The Political Economy of Demographic Change*, London: Heinemann

Finer, M (1974) *Report of the Committee on One-Parent Families*, London: HMSO

Francome, C (1994) *The Great Leap: A Study of 107 Hindu and Sikh Students*, London: Middlesex University

Giddens, A (1992) *The Transformation of Intimacy*, Cambridge: Polity Press

Haskey, J (1993) 'Trends in Numbers of One-Parent Families', *Population Trends*, 71

Hylton, C (1997) *Family Survival Strategies*, A Moyenda Black Families Talking Project, London: Exploring Parenthood

Institute of Public Policy Research (IPPR) (1997) *A Report on a Survey Conducted by NOP*, London: Institute of Public Policy Research

James-Fergus, S (1997) 'Rebuilding the African-Caribbean Community in Britain' in G Dench (ed) (1997)

Joshi, H (1989) (ed) *The Changing Population of Britain*, Oxford: Blackwell

Kiernan, K and Eastaugh, V (1993) *Cohabitation, Extra-marital Childrearing and Social Policy*, London: Family Policy Studies Centre

Land, H (1969) *Large Families in London*, London: George Bell

McRae, S (1993) *Cohabiting Mothers: Changing Marriage and Motherhood*, London: Policy Studies Institute

McRae, S (1997) 'Household and Labour Market Change: Implications for the Growth of Inequality in Britain', *British Journal of Sociology*, 48 (3).

Metcalf, H, Modood, T and Virdee, S (1996) *Asian Self Employment: The Interaction of Culture and Economics*, London: Policy Studies Institute

Modood, T (1998) 'Anti-Essentialism, Multiculturalism and the "Recognition" of Religious Minorities', *Journal of Political Philosophy*, 6 (3)

Modood, T, Beishon, S and Virdee, S (1994) *Changing Ethnic Identities*, London: Policy Studies Institute

Modood, T, Berthoud, R, Lakey, J, Nazroo, J, Smith, P, Virdee, S and Beishon, S (1997) *Ethnic Minorities in Britain: Diversity and Disadvantage*, London: Policy Studies Institute

Parekh, B (1995) 'Cultural Pluralism and the Limits of Diversity', *Alternatives*, 20

Smart, C (1997) 'Wishful Thinking and Harmful Tinkering? Sociological Reflections on Family Policy', *British Journal of Social Policy*, (26), 3

Song, M and Edwards, R (1996) 'Comment: Raising Questions About Perspectives on Black Lone Motherhood', *British Journal of Social Policy*

UK Action Committee on Islamic Affairs (UKACIA) (1997) *Elections 1997 and British Muslims: For a Fair and Caring Society*, UKACIA